supermom

Celebrating All of Who You Are

supermom

Celebrating All of Who You Are

Shevaughn D. Henderson
Certified Women's Empowerment Coach

Rising Sunset Publishing
A Literary and Music Publishing Company

Copyright © 2019 by Shevaughn D. Henderson

All rights reserved. In accordance with the U.S. Copyright Act of 1976, the scanning, uploading, and electronic sharing of any part of this book without permission of the publisher is an unlawful piracy and theft of the author's intellectual property. If you would like to use material from this book, other than for book review purposes, written permission must be given prior to use by the publisher at thesupermocoach@gmail.com, Attn: Permissions. Thank you in advance for your support of the author's rights.

Shevaughn Henderson
ATTN: Permissions
info@sd-henderson.com
www.sd-henderson.com

Ordering Information

Individual Sales. Available through retailers & ePub available on author website at sd-henderson.com.

Scripture quotation taken from the Holy Bible New International Version® NIV®

Copyright © 1973,1978, 1984, 2011by Biblica, Inc.™

Used by permission. All rights reserved worldwide.

First Printing: 2019

Cover Design: Shevaughn D. Henderson

ISBN 978-0-578-50088-1

♥ ♥ ♥ ♥

To my children Omari, Matthew, Jasmine, and Zoey.
I will always be your Supermom!!

Praise for Supermom

"I found the book to be very good and I was able to connect to the things that were written. I was reminded of myself in many instances. I would recommend this book to all women young and old. Lots of insight."

~ Mary Hinton, Retired Teacher & Mom of 2 and grandma

Contents

Preface	09

Part One: The New Mom

Chapter 1: The Transition	13
Chapter 2: Accepting Your New Position	27
Chapter 3: Learning How to Be You	41
Chapter 4: The Everyday Guide	51

Part Two: Celebrating All of Who We Are

Chapter 5: Owning Supermom	61
Chapter 6: Managing Motherhood	67
Chapter 7: A Woman First	77
Chapter 8: Unending Love	85

Part Three: Bridging the Gap

Chapter 9: Our Views of Each Other	93
Chapter 10: Embracing the Sisterhood	103
Chapter 11: One Mother at a Time	111

Part Four: Mom to Supermom

Chapter 12: Dream	121
Chapter 13: Believe	137
Chapter 14: Live	149
Quotes to Remember	157
Afterword	159
Bible Verses	161
Notes	163
Acknowledgements	165
About the Author	169

Preface

    Written for the woman of today's society. Where the need for women of all ages, backgrounds and socioeconomic status to stand together is in high demand. Reaching new heights in our day in age. For years, women have talked behind each other's back about other women. Women putting each other down for what they perceive a mother's behavior should be. Society places an unrealistic expectation on mothers that cannot be met by some individuals. Not because of their lack of the want. However, it is due to their lack in ability and their socioeconomic restraints.

    There are some common core behaviors all people should adhere to when in a common area amongst other individuals. Being respectful of yourself and of others is first and foremost. In what should be a given for all, is often not. Teaching a child to respect their elders and others is a lesson taught in the generation that preceded us. In which, should have stuck with the now mothers in how we treat each other as adults now.

Is this an issue we should degrade another woman for? Is it an issue we should degrade our self for?

It is beyond time for the understanding that we are all mothers doing the best that we can. There isn't a better way to parent a child. However, if we as women have the knowledge to not judge one another, we will be better off as a society. There is always room for improvement. Indeed, mothers share stories and experiences all the time. It is then, in that moment, that we should consider helping one another when needed. We need to be that role model that children need to see in today's society. We all need to be loving, caring, and accepting of new ideas. Don't you think it is time to break the mold?

PART ONE

New Mom Struggles

1

The Transition

In today's day in age women don't often take time to consider how we came about with respect to having children. Sure, we know the science behind the how. But, how does our mind interpret the when and how we react when it does happen? How far back does your subconscious go? Back to a time when you were a child? That is one thing I believe happens when we think about having children.

I believe our mind goes back to when we were children. Thinking of the time when life was simple and you had ideas of how you were going to be as a mother. Growing up as young girls, we often play with toys that represent household items. For instance, baby dolls equipped with buggy, pots and pans, and other child size toys. This is when we as little girls have the chance to practice becoming a mother, a mother to our baby dolls.

Another way to interpret it would be, playing house. Initially, you can see in their eyes the joy they have when they are rocking their baby to sleep. You can often bond with these young girls during this experience as a mother or even an aunt. Teaching a young girl how to properly hold her baby doll during playtime is when she can learn how to become mother herself.

Mimicking what she sees at home, is how she will portray onto her baby doll. There are some young girls that do not initially have the desire to want to play with baby dolls. And of course, that is perfectly fine. They prefer to play with other toys that intrigue their interest, such as sports toys. The drive to play sports is at the forefront. Like all children, they will have plenty of time to discover who they are and in whom they will be.

One thing we can do as women is ensure our children are equipped with the knowledge and the know-how. For everything is passed down from the mother. In studying race relations and how traditions were passed down is the moment I realized how important our roles are as women and mothers.

Ensuring children have a good role model is of the most importance. Whether it be their own mother, aunt, or babysitter it is very important to the developmental stage of young girls. As we all know, eventually, all young girls will grow up and her time of playing with baby dolls will end.

When the boys start noticing her, she is either going to feel self-confident or it may take her some time to come into her own. Either way, during this stage of development can leave lasting effects on her self-esteem. A young lady is very impressionable. It is our jobs as women to stand up and be the role models they need for us to make sure we are raising young confident women.

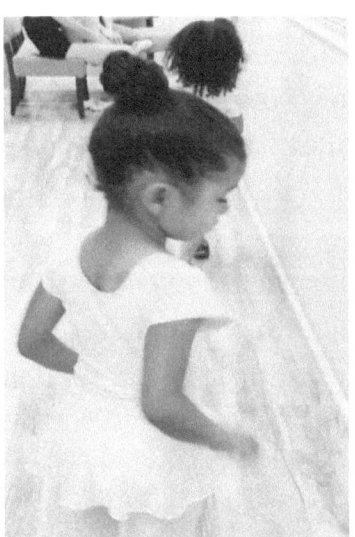

Figure 1.1 "Self-Image"

How do we do that? It all starts at home. Who we let hang around our children? What we let them watch on television? Raising our children with great values and self-respect. Also, by remembering that growing up is more challenging to some girls than others. With the right guidance for her, she can soar to her hearts desires.

The 1950's Standard

In a perfect world, a young lady will find a nice boy and settle down to have children of her own. Take for instance, the old standard of living for the women to whom preceded our generation. Dating and committing oneself to a young man by marriage is the 1950's idea any parent would want their child to do, should they have that mentality. The 1950's concept of marriage that I am referring to is meeting that special someone, getting married and having those two children right after marriage. Few and far in between hold onto that marriage concept and proceed to do just that.

Marry their college sweetheart, that significant other they met at the grocery store, or perhaps that one from that online dating site they used and didn't think anything would come from it. Yes, it does happen, not as often as we may think. However, we know there are some parents that are more opened minded about relationships in general. Wanting the best for your child is what matters to them in the end. As do all parents, because like we know first-hand this world is less than perfect.

Today's society has seemed to stray away from the 1950's marriage concept and adapted the 'Single Parent' concept. Why? Society has made it more acceptable to be a single parent. Mainstream media has replaced the television shows of the era that depicted the 1950's marriage/family model with shows they felt were more functional of how they saw society. Television shows that are supposed to be based on "reality" rather than "wholesome" television shows. Perhaps, as people got older and started analyzing the television shows that depicted the 1950's marriage model and their portrayal of an image of family that was not true to form for most families.

I know I thought it was how a marriage should be. A happily married couple with kids, a good job for the husband while the mom stayed at home tending to the house and kids. However, it was far from my reality at the time and in today's times. But, it was something I wanted and wanted to try and obtain for myself. However, not all women or men feel the same way I do and that's perfectly fine. As we know it is ultimately their decision. One thing to remember is it does not matter what our thoughts are on the matter of marriage. Our thoughts and convictions on marriage can be and are very different.

For many individualized reasons, people are less likely to stay in relationships that do not work for the sake of the child as how it was done in the 1950's. Indeed, that is something that only they can determine for themselves.

A Blessing to Come

There comes a time when you will be blessed with an undeniable blessing. Whether you are a married woman or a single woman, being blessed to have a child is a beautiful thing. It could be at the beginning of a marriage, dating, or possibly before a couple says, "I Do." However, your journey to motherhood began, it can become the most precious moment of all. In all honesty, my start to motherhood came before I expected. In planning my life with my now husband, we were not expecting to have a child prior to marriage. But, *when you do grown up things, grown up things happen.* Truly it can be a defining moment in a couple's relationship. Sometimes for the better, sometimes for the worst.

In your steps to becoming a mother, you will experience all aspects of the playing field, from different types emotions to the ever so popular weight gain. You will be amazed at the amount of emotions you will experience as that special day arrives.

Your "plan" may not be to have a child for quite some time. Perhaps, you never thought of yourself going through this while in college, during your first year of marriage. I assure you when the day of that missed period comes you will feel some type of way.

The wonder, the not knowing "Am I pregnant?" The first initial reaction you have is "OH-MY-G**! Am I really going through this right now?" Hopefully, you will have a happy sense of the reaction as these thoughts go through your head. Excitement building up and thoughts of "how am I going to tell David about us expecting?

"Should I surprise him?"

"Maybe I should buy a baby blanket and give it to him."

These are all very exciting things to think about as your mind goes through this phase of becoming a parent. However, not everyone experiences these happy feelings at first.

Some women may experience feeling of fright as they hear the news they are going to become a parent. Many of these feelings of fright come from experiences that they may have seen people they know go through. Ideas they could have got from a movie or simply from a childhood experience they had. However, once the initial shock has set in, it is time to confront these feelings and confirm your suspicions by seeing your doctor. If that doctor appointment is a few days out, it may be wise to grab that home pregnancy test and take the plunge.

On your way, there you may even try to convince yourself that you are not pregnant. "I'm really not pregnant. It must be a false alarm." "I couldn't be pregnant."

Once you get to the doctor's office, don't let those overwhelming feelings hit you. You will be fine either way the cookie is sliced. The doctor may then proceed to ask you "Do you want to be pregnant?" For a quick minute, you have to ask yourself that very question. Uttering the word "yes," in fright, excitement and even out of obligation because you don't want the doctor to think badly about a woman who came in for a pregnancy test and doesn't want to be pregnant. Right?

"Well, great" the doctor answers "because you are pregnant!" Excited and scared, you leave the doctor's office with other official "Yes!" Now you can start preparing for that bundle of joy. It is a wonderful feeling to be able to experience the transition of becoming a mother. The weight gain, the swollen feet and ankles, the morning sickness. Yeah right! It's not as cut and dry for most women. Even when you are excited to become a mother. The symptoms can easily sour your mood. It's good to know that you are not alone. Many women have faced that same issue. You will get through it, you just have to have *faith* and *faith in yourself*.

Just imagine though, your whole life is now beginning to change. You don't even realize how much.

Now that you have had some time to sit with the idea of becoming a parent, excitement will fill your heart in an overwhelming amount. As excitement begins to build between you and your significant other, you will want to share the joyous news with family and friends. It's time to send out that mass notice over social media waves and phone calls.

The Transition

Once you are expecting, from anyone to everyone has advice of how you should raise your child. Be that as it may, most of them do come from a genuine place from the heart. However, it can be a scary thing. Motherhood is a full-time job. There are no ten-minute breaks, lunchtime breaks, or bathroom breaks. Yes, I said it. No bathroom breaks. *Remember, you were entrusted with a brand-new life to love, raise and support and what a blessing that is.*

Children will hunt you down, all the way to the bathroom. Yes, as soon as that beautiful bouncing bundle of joy arrives, you go from a carefree woman to a full-time caregiver for a tiny version of you. It is both scary and wonderful all wrapped into one.

> *Being a mother is a full-time job.*

Don't get me wrong. I truly accepted this position as a gift and blessing. It is the very essence of learning how to deal with the transition from who you thought you were to the person you are now going to become.

This very milestone can make or break you. The transition from woman to mother is a very deep and emotional experience. Your hormones are changing and the different levels of hormones can cause a woman to experience Postpartum Depression and 'Baby Blues' to name a few. How you manage the transition from being pregnant to motherhood can be life altering.

First, let's give you some concrete definitions of the different types of hormonal changes that I have mentioned. According to the U.S. National Library of Medicine, *Postpartum Depression* is a moderate to severe depression in a woman after she has given birth. Postpartum Depression may occur right after delivery or up to a year later. They state that postpartum depression occurs within the first three months after delivery. *

Causes of postpartum depression range from the changes in your body forma the pregnancy and delivery, lack of sleep, social/work relationships, less time for yourself, and worries about your ability to be a good mother. There are also some factors that may put you at a higher risk. For instance, having a history of depression, being under the age of 20, taking illegal substances, smoking and many others. For a full list of the risk factors and symptoms, please speak with your physician or you can go to the U.S. National Library of Medicine.

'Baby Blues' is defined as a heightened emotional state that can affect eight or more new moms in the first days after giving birth. * Baby Blues gradually subsides within a couple of weeks. Generally, baby blues can go untreated with medication. Having the baby blues can be common and getting help is key to getting you, the mother, out of the fragile emotional state.

I had baby blues with my first son. I placed unrealistic expectations of what I thought a mother

The Transition

should be. Wanting to be "the perfect mother" was one of my ideas. I thought my son would be like other newborns I heard about. I thought he would be sleeping at night and wide awake during the day. I had no idea or expectation that my idea could potentially cause me to experience something that could be harmful to me emotionally. I had to quickly realize there is no such thing as "the perfect mother." It is normal to make mistakes because your child does not come with a manual.

Throughout the course of my baby blues, I resented my husband for going to work and leaving me alone with our son. I thought my husband should have done more for me so I could sleep. Granted, he was working full-time and had time off the first few weeks of my son's birth. Of course, that's fine for your spouse to go to work. They do have to continue to support the family. But, he still had to wake me up because I had to breastfeed. It wasn't until I spoke my frustrations to a coworker during a visit to show off the baby and get out of the house that she informed me about the 'baby blues' and said I needed to tell my doctor.

Figure 1.2 "The Perfect Mother"

It was a huge relief to know something wasn't wrong with me. I wasn't a bad mother for feeling these things. It helped to talk to someone about how I was feeling. I chose to talk to someone whose opinion I trusted. Everything would be all right as soon as I get myself some help. Indeed, it took me about two weeks to get over the dramatic hormonal changes I was going through. I could do that by removing the unrealistic expectations I placed on myself and be the best mother I could be.

I had to learn to place my son on a schedule so I could get some sleep and he could learn to sleep at the correct time of day for my family. It was not an easy task. However, he learned to stick to the schedule and has been on a schedule ever since.

Now that I have given you concrete definitions of these types of disorders you could be facing as a new mother, let me remind you how important it is to speak with your health provider and keep an eye on your health during your transition through motherhood.

> *If you are experiencing any signs of depression, please contact your doctor immediately. If you experience any of the following symptoms please Call 911 or get immediate emergency help:*
> *** Having Hallucinations & delusions about yourself or your baby.*
> *** You have thoughts about hurting yourself or your baby.*

These are very serious issues that need immediate attention for your sake and your baby's. It may also help to inform a family member so they can give moral support as you are going through a trying time. Although, I have mentioned the transition of pregnancy to motherhood, there is one topic we can't forget to mention as we speak on motherhood, Adoption.

There are women out there that have a heart big enough to spread their love around and take it upon themselves to open their home to a child that is not their biological child. Although, they do not partake in the childbearing experience, it doesn't lessen their ability or their heart to raise a child. Remember, children don't need material items, they only need the love to grow.

> *Good parenting has nothing to do with DNA.*

Depending on the age of the child these mothers adopt, will depend on if they have a lot of sleepless nights. I'm sure in some cases children can't sleep in a new environment, and that is a task all in its self. Either way, an adoptive parent has the other transitions that they experience before they can bring their child home. I commend them for choosing to embark on parenthood. There are a lot of children out there that need a good home. These women have stepped up to do just that.

Chapter Summary

- We mimic what we see at home.

- A good role model is important.

- Children are a blessing.

- You were entrusted to *love, raise,* and *support* your child.

- *Motherhood* is a full-time job.

- "The Perfect Mother" does not exist. So, don't be afraid to make mistakes.

2

Accepting Your New Position

Hurray!! You are a new mother. Welcome to a *sisterhood* of motherhood. It is a blessing to be able to experience the joy that having a child can bring. Now that you are a mom that has been doing this awhile, it is time to see if you truly accept your new position in life. I understand that many of you may think you have truly accepted it without question and you may have. However, let's think long and hard about that word "accept." There are a few things to consider while you think about your position as a mother.

Are you walking in the *joy* of motherhood? Are you stressed out? Are you upset you can't go out as much as you used to do before? These are all questions we as women should be asking ourselves. Do we get upset that some of our friends don't want to call us to go out any more because we have a new baby? Heck, they may not even want to call you to go out with them because you may have kids at home period and they're single without kids. Does that upset you? These are all thought provoking questions you should ask yourself. Really digging deep inside your being in understanding your position in motherhood can really take you further in your understanding as a woman and individual.

In considering this concept of acceptance, think also about who you are as a mother and the true sense of the word accept.

Acceptance

As we transition through any new phase or journey in life, accepting who we are in the new sense of the word will dictate how we further ourselves for our future. Whether we fight it or take it head on and add this new peace to our mold of ourselves. For instance, it is like a pot made of clay. In taking a pottery class, you would start off with a piece of clay and water and work the clay to shape and mold it in what you may think to be a work of art. If someone were to accidentally bump into you while you were molding this work of art, it would change the design of the pot.

Now you have the choice of accepting their apology and going on with the now changed design of the clay or you can decide to add more water and clay to reshape it or simply start over. Either way it is now a different journey you are on in molding this piece of clay. Being content in who you are is just as this metaphor of designing this piece of clay. Accepting all of who you are faults and all is vital to your growth not only as a mother, but as an individual. In life, there is always going to be some bumps in the road that may take us in an alternate direction. Accepting the challenge to use what life has given us and turn it into something that will make us even more beautiful inside our soul to shine in us and through us is the journey we are all going through.

    A concept I know all too well. It took myself some time to adjust to the new lifestyle I had. I was totally fine with the whole "mom" thing. I got this down pat. I was a very overprotective mama lioness. I worked, made sure my husband and baby were all taken care of. That was the easy part of my new position. What I had the problem with was accepting that I had to change other habits of mine.

    Like going to get my nails done, spending nonsense time and money of myself. Not that it's a big deal as I look back at this. But, at the time that's all I used to do. I didn't ever have to take care of anyone else but me. I didn't accept the fact that I felt like I could no longer be selfish and overspend on things that seemed so minuscule. It was more of the having to "change" in general. I felt like I was going to lose who I was because I didn't fully comprehend the world of change. I hated change for a very long time. Change did not come easy for me.

As a kid, I always hated progression into a new school chapter in my life. Why? Change. I am not one to throw a party for change. For years, it was something I had to work on. Deep down inside some of us, myself included, think it's a bad thing to change. When in essence, it's not change, its *growth*. God has taught me this lesson over and over until I finally understood it was ok to change and grow. I like to say it was a lesson I had to learn four times. Hence, the four children I now have. I was a little hard-headed when it came to surrendering my all. *It truly coincides with allowing yourself to let go, accept the wholeness of who you are and believe in yourself to be a great mother.*

Parenting styles sometimes can change with anyone trying to learn something new or by simply mimicking someone you see in whom you admire their skills. Have you changed your style of parenting to fight what you may think the "norm" should be? Have you shopped around for moms that are "perfect?" Exhausted yourself and your finances to respond to the "mom" mentality? That's what we do when we go *searching* for what is already in us to do. Believing in ourselves is half the battle. Believing we can conquer the world as a mom and woman comes with an inner connection to our spirituality.

I believe that *95% of parenting in leading by example, the other 5% is life*, by meaning of world experiences. The battle in parenting is making sure you are in the lead in teaching your child right from wrong. Don't get me wrong. It is great to live and to learn as the old saying goes. But, in all perspective to the world, being grounded in family before you venture out and start living helps you in understanding the world. Plus, if you live your life to the fullest, you will show your child how it's done. Teaching them how to be strong and full of the spirit of life as you are.

A further look at the word *accept* as the key to your growth inside this new role of your life. A concept not fully used by a wide majority of both women and men in many topics in life. For instance, let's say you are having a mild disagreement with your spouse. In this disagreement, you know without a shadow of a doubt you are right. If your spouse goes in the right directions of acceptance, he will agree with you and your disagreement is over. But, if your spouse chooses to go in the opposite direction of accept, you two can possibly go down the path of WWIII. However, depending on if you are willing to stick to your guns just for the sake of proving you are right and winning an argument. It could turn into something you had no intention of giving life to. Like majority of relationships, this will happen several times because you have two different personalities at work here.

What it all comes down to is how you are built inside. Allowing yourself to be human and make mistakes but knowing it's okay to take on a new role in life to help get you where you need to be.

Asking Questions

As you are going through your journey of becoming a mother, it is important to ask questions. Ask questions to people you know, friends and family that have been through this stage prior to you. Some people also consider asking their child's pediatrician. The pediatrician is a great person to ask concerning your child's health. However, if it is a question regarding a non-life threatening issue it may be better to ask someone that is closer to home. Asking someone you know and trust for information. Then you can best decide if it is something you would like to do or if you would still rather call the doctor. They know and understand how new mothers are. The burning questions they may have. I know they are more than happy to help with any questions concerning you regarding your child.

When I was in this stage of motherhood, I left some questions that could wait and wrote them on a sheet of paper and placed it in my son's diaper bag for myself as a new mom not to forget it at the next doctor appointment. As an infant, they have plenty of back to back well baby checkups to insure they are growing the way they should be growing.

As I mentioned before, if your child is having an issue, then call the pediatrician immediately. They can advise you in what to do next.

That proved to be what I needed to do with my first born. There was an issue I wasn't sure if he was starting to look yellow. I was worried he may be getting jaundice. The pediatrician said his levels were a little low when he was first born. However, his levels did go up. His pediatrician said to be on the safe side, let him get a little sun light near the window and she would check on him in a couple of days. That's exactly what I did, as a worried mother, I held him near the window for a little at a time, and he was fine.

At that time, my worries were not over. At five months old, my first-born infant couldn't keep his food down. Everything he ate, came right back up. I immediately called the pediatrician. Being that it was a weekend, she had a plan in place for parents that called on the weekend. A voicemail would be left, she would be paged with your call and voicemail. I was advised to take him to the nearest hospital.

The emergency room doctor was the only one available that evening. Their pediatricians were not in that night. There had been a bug going around and the doctor suggested it was that and to go home and be sure to follow up with his pediatrician on Monday. Two days later at our follow-up doctor visit, his doctor found a problem in his abdomen when she felt around checking his stomach area for any abnormalities.

She told me she couldn't be one hundred percent sure unless she had an x-ray to what may be wrong. She told me she was going to write what she suspected on her prescription pad and to hand it to the ER doctor. Waiting for x-rays for a private doctor's office would have taken too long. Time was of the essence. For my son's sake, the doctor advised me not to go to the hospital he went to previously. "Take him to the hospital that is on your insurance card," she replied.

Worried and scared, my husband and I proceeded to drive him to the hospital. Upon calling his name I told the doctor his primary doctor wrote him a note. They immediately sent him for x-ray's. As the ER doctor thought he saw what his primary doctor suspected, he called on the advice of the top-notch pediatrician at their hospital. Scheduled to go home, the emergency room doctor got to him before he left and asked to consult.

Luckily for us, he didn't go home just yet. He consulted, it was what his primary pediatrician suspected. They immediately transferred my son to the Miller's Children's Hospital in Long Beach, California. One of the best children's hospitals in our state. Ironically, this children's hospital is located right next to the emergency room we had just visited when this whole ordeal started.

My five-month-old son was diagnosed with an intussusception and we were told he needed surgery. For those of you who may not know what an intussusception is, it is where a part of the intestine telescopes inside itself. In some cases, it can be corrected without surgery. However, for my little man it was in a place where it had to be surgically removed.

It was the most horrifying ordeal I could have went through as a new mother.

The importance in this scenario is the fact that I knew something was off and wasn't right with my son. I had my intuition and as a mother/parent you will know deep down inside your soul. More importantly, when you get that urging gut feeling, don't ignore it. You will never know anything in life if you don't ask questions. If that isn't the best lesson in life, God gives us these feelings for a reason. The reason to protect us from harm and I truly believe that.

Understanding Who You Are

In understanding who we are as women and mothers, a major question to ask to yourself is are you "truly happy?" Understanding your happiness will help insure you do not lose yourself in "being mom." Placing unrealistic boundaries on yourself can make it harder for you to keep up with your "idea" of what a mother should be, rather than just being who you are. A great thing to do and remember is to relax. Taking a deep breath in and out to help steady your mind and emotions is a great place to start.

Getting into some exercise that is good for your health and well-being is a way to help you relax. For instance, Yoga. Yoga is a good place to go for helping you find your Chi. If you don't know what Chi is it is the life force in which circulates in the body. To build up your Chi, there is an exercise that promotes this, Tai Chi.

Finding a hormonal balance is something that I am trying in my life to help balance me out. As a Libra, I love balance naturally. I have been listening and focusing on the Lord and finding my peace and understanding how to maintain it daily. I have also tried some yoga exercises. I am not an expert. But, I think it's something I can try on more than a couple occasions.

Another way to help you relax is to set goals, realistic goals with a short time frame. For instance, "I want to make sure I try to get the baby on a sleep schedule." If it doesn't happen right away don't worry. Take a deep breath and keep trying and the baby will eventually get it when it is ready. All this means is you should stay strong and go with their flow.

Why a short time frame? It doesn't place too much pressure on you to accomplish a big task. When we attack tasks in pieces it helps us to get through it in an orderly fashion. It doesn't overwhelm you by placing unnecessary stress on your shoulders. As we break tasks down, our brain processes them easier. It won't throw you into a panic by looking at all the steps in a task at one time.

Now that we know why our brain can't process a massive task, we can be surely rest that it is okay to want to break down a task to a more manageable size.

So, we can conquer it and then some. What is that old saying? Small victories when wars.

You are not alone in the sleep deprivation area. Making sure your child is on a sleep schedule is an issue I know all too well. I have had the sleepless nights' issue will all four of my children. Yes, all four of my children. Did I mention I had a hard time with accepting my loss of sleep? Well, I was right there with you. But, you should remember, you had to learn to do things that were new to you and so does your baby.

I will be honest. It took me a minute to come to grips with that concept with each child I had. Yes, I said with each child. It was hard for someone like me. Only for one reason, I love to get my full eight hours of sleep. A little background on that, being an only child there was never any other siblings to wake me up and have fun. You know the usual sibling stuff. I would stay up late on the weekends with my grandmother and being the grandmother that she was the "I will let my grand baby do what she wants," to an extent, the grandma rules kind of thing. She never pressed the issue to wake me up at a certain time. Which, was right up my alley and of course not my mother's idea. So, when I had my children, I was still living the sleep until 10 am kind of thing because I worked at night.

Having this kind of background of "extra" sleep time, it took a while to break my old habit that took many years to build. I was always thrown for a curve ball with that issue with each child. You do have to be ready for your baby to not cooperate right away. Like the old saying goes, better safe than sorry. On the other hand, you may be the one to say, "I have been lucky in that department." If that's you, that's awesome!

These different challenges with you as a new mother can be daunting. But, don't let it discourage you. Whether your challenge is getting the full eight hours of sleep or a challenge of getting used to the new routine of life, you will be just fine. *It is our perseverance and faith that gets us through the difficulties.*

Chapter Summary

- Know the significance of "accept"

- Walk in the joy of motherhood

- Ask questions when you are uncertain

- Listen to your intuition

- Set realistic goals

- Relax

3

Learning How to Be You

Becoming a mother is life changing. It can often affect how we view our self-image as a mother and a woman. Life of course is not all about self-image. However, we know that how we are as women and how society plays apart in the way they view woman in general.

We often spend time asking ourselves some hard questions as we evaluate our life course. Am I a good mother? How should I dress now that I am a mom? Will I be like my mother? With these hard questions, we may start to express some not so needed self-doubt. "I'm going to make mistakes." "I am not Supermom. I can't possibly do the all the things a Supermom does." "I am not like that mom over there. Why is she so calm, cool and collected?"

As I mentioned in Chapter 1, there is no such thing as a "perfect mother." But, let me also tell you that you are *perfect* for your child. You were given the opportunity to love this tiny little person and they do not place any type of judgement on you. They don't know that you don't know how to sew. They don't know you don't have a green thumb. Whatever it is that you think you "should" know how to do, they don't care.

Their only concern is that you love them and by how you express this love is all they care about. You could have all the money in the world and all that would come with that, but, the only thing that would matter to them is the unconditional love and support from you. Like the old saying my mother and grandmother would say is, you can't buy love.

If you are not confident in who you are as a woman and mother comparison will creep in. Comparing yourself to other women and mothers is a huge sign of self-doubt and low self-esteem. Comparison along with a social issue, can be your worst nightmare. Looking at the mothers that "have it all together," so you think. At least that is what you may tell yourself if you don't watch your own self-image. Your view of your own self-image shapes the way you parent your child.

Let me elaborate on that idea. If you are constantly studying what another mother is doing, you too will find yourself imitating her behavior and how she parents her children. I am not saying don't converse with other mothers about what questions you have and advice they may be able to give to you. I am here to say that it is important you pay attention to everything that *shapes your view*.

Learning to be consciously aware of how you were brought up as a child can assist you in raising your own child. Some of you may be thinking you do not want to think of yourself as turning into your mother. I know and I understand that idea. I sure didn't want to consider that idea myself when I first became a mother. Not because she was a bad mother. But, because of the old stigma that was placed on women in the past. Like being like your mother is a bad thing. On the contrary, it is through the mother that traditions are passed down and how to take care of your home and family comes through the mother. I know there have been times where I have said something or did something that reminded me of my mother. Honestly, when I do it makes me laugh.

Figure 3.1 "Your View"

Whether your mother was the best mother or the worst mother in your eyes, we need to lean on an understanding that she did the best she could with what she was able to do. Using everything she did can be a useful learning tool for you. From the mistakes to the days she was at her best, we as mothers ourselves must utilize all the tools we were given and grow from there. In thinking of parenting, it all comes to leading our children through the examples we give them. When I think about life and parenting, as I mentioned in chapter 2, my belief is that 95% of parenting is leading by example the other 5% is life. The battle is making sure you, as a parent, are in the lead and not life. Yes, life lessons can be great. But, we also need to realize that our children are better off learning from us at home first. We need to be that standard of morals and let them grow from there.

"I took you from the ends of the earth, from its farthest corners I called you I said, 'You are my servant'; I have chosen you and have not rejected you. So do not fear, for I am with you; do not be dismayed, for I am your God. I will strengthen you and help you; I will uphold you with my righteous right hand."
Isaiah 41:9-10 NIV®

In trying to understand my heart and becoming a mother, this scripture has helped me in feeling confident in my role as a mother. You were chosen to be a mother. I was chosen to be a mother. It is a role we need to be confident in. In the days when we are not, its ok. This is when we need to embrace all of who we are regardless of our faults. Remembering that we are a child of God first. Resting upon that idea you can rest assure, you were not mistaken in becoming a mother.

Building Your Community

An important part of motherhood is having a reliable community to count on when you need it. My definition of a community is a group of family and friends that share a common interest. The common interest that they genuinely care about you and your family's well-being. This will help you in the coming years as your child grows. You will be able to call on the people you have in your community for advice.

As you are defining your close net community, it is important to have people that have children as well as people who don't.

Let's say you have a friend that has a child in your community. This friend can be a point of reference when you are feeling unsure about something. You two can share life experiences and she can offer encouragement. Being an encouragement and receiving encouragement is a good thing.

Having someone to sow seeds of encouragement to you is good for any stage of motherhood you are in. *Why?* It helps to ease the mind and body of the mother. It doesn't help mothers only. It is a life lesson that can be passed on to your children. In fact, being open to giving encouragement on a regular basis to your friends and family in your community will spark the same encouragement in them as it has in you.

Both encouragement and a point of reference are not the only asset in a healthy community of friends and family. They are also a great lead to building great friendships with others. A lesson that can be taught to your children. Children not only learn from actual hands on teaching. They learn from watching our actions as parents. Teaching our children how to build friendships through our actions is a great way to build up their self-confidence. For instance, if we do not teach them how to interact with others, how do they learn.

Taking that step out in faith is a huge thing to do for anyone. Ensuring that we do, we give our children an extra ordinary lead in building mechanisms they will need later in life. If we don't do our part, they could end up not picking up that tactic as fast as we would like, leaving them open to loneliness. A trait that no parent wants to see their child go through. Heck. For adults, it can be stressful and detrimental to our lives.

Play Dates

Play dates are a great way to get your child out there and social. When it's time to schedule their first play date, sometimes it can be a little nerve wracking. How are

"We were created to be social human beings."

they going to react to each other? Is my baby going to get along well with other kids? Are the kids nice? What will happen if that kids hits my child? Is the parent going to say something?

All these questions can come up along with others. However, scheduling a play date with mothers you know will be a great way to socialize your child. It is in our very nature that we interact with other people. We cannot keep our children locked up in the house because of what may happen. An idea many parents have joked about in conversation.

"I'm locking up my daughter in the house until she's eighteen."

"My daughter is going to stay home until she gets married."

Ideas and jokes that are not very realistic. It is funny the way we do reference keeping the kids in the house until they are adults, it is always regarding our daughters. An unrealistic act as parents we would not want to do. All because of the fears of the world.

Nervous? Don't be. There is no need to be nervous. We all feel the same way. We all want our children to be safe and healthy.

In that manner, we need to think about socialization of our child/children. It is both healthy for our child and for us. Think about it. No interaction for your child and what it can lead to. As I just mentioned loneliness is a huge factor. Also, stress. Being stressful is not healthy. Let alone becoming a stressful child. Not interacting with other children can cause stress in some children. Not all children are affected in that way. You should ask yourself a question. Is that a risk you are willing to take?

It will be just fine. The benefits of assisting your child in building friendships is worth the anxiety of the first play date. There are benefits for you as a new mother. It will give you some grown-up time with other parents and moms.

Teaching the value of good friendships is a great life lesson for your child. In watching you interact with another mother, your child is depositing seeds of wisdom into what I refer to as a "friendship bank."

A friendship bank is part of the system inside your whole being that can differentiate what a friend is. It connects to your mind, body, and soul. The *mind* understands what a friend is. The *body* knows how to react when you see your friend. The *soul* feels all its emotions with every part of interaction of your friendship.

Babysitters

In building your community, it is important to establish a list of babysitters. The importance of a good quality babysitter will matter to you when you need it most. For instance, there will be a time that you want to enjoy some adult time. A night out with the hubby or a girlfriend for some time alone away from your baby. That person will matter before you know it.

You will need to start putting in the foot work on establishing an agreement with a family member, friend, or simply someone that comes highly recommended. For two reasons. First and foremost, you want dependability. You want to know that someone in your community will be able to help you out when you truly need it. Secondly, you won't be able to do what you need to do if those steps are not taken prior to having to do anything.

Someone that comes highly recommended is a person referred by a family member or friend. Someone in whom you trust may use this person for their babysitter needs.

I have done this very thing. Moving closer to the in-laws left me without anyone I know to watch my children. I relied on my sister-in-law to refer someone she used to watch my children. I did have to see how my children reacted to meeting her so I will know if they would be comfortable with a new babysitter. Fortunately, there was nothing to worry about. My children warmed up to her nicely. They were introduced to her. For our first job, they were with their cousins that knew her well. I will say it helped them to have their cousins on their first new babysitter experience. That may not always happen. I suggest letting your child get to know this new person by seeing them and interacting with the new sitter prior to the actual day.

Chapter Summary

- Know how to recognize self-doubt.

- Self-Image shapes how we parent.

- You were chosen to become a mother.

- Build a reliable community

- "We were created to be social human beings."

- Teaching the value of a good friendship is a great life lesson.

4

The Everyday Guide

Going through the motions is what it can feel like when we think of an everyday guide or routine. The endless routine of waking up gathering your clothes, coffee, kids to get ready for what the day is going to be like. Depending on your family size and work environment/status will depend on how you get through your day. Ultimately, isn't that just it though. We are going through our daily lives. The thing is, are we *allowing* ourselves to just go through the *motions,* subconsciously, not realizing we are doing it or are we living our lives with an *expectancy* of great things?

Living with an expectancy can be a great key to success for mothers and individuals in general. What type of expectancy am I speaking of? An expectancy of a positive attitude. A positive attitude for having a great day for yourself and your family. Sure, life happens, but, if we go about our daily routines with an expectancy of a delightful day for our own standards,

A routine is not only good for your child, it is also we won't be taken off guard too much when the unexpected happens. Our own standards can be different for every one of us.

I can't tell you my standards for your life because I'm not living your life. You must determine what that means for you and your family. For instance, if you have a child that usually gives you a hard time to get up for school, expecting to have a great day can mean for you that they got up and dress for school with no hassle to you. Personally, that is a challenge and expectancy I deal with on a day to day basis. With four children, everyone's internal time clock is different.

An expectancy of strength, for the times of need when you are having a bad day. The baby didn't let you sleep the night before. Expectant of having strength can give you that extra oomph you need to attack your day.

Expectancy of joy for the day. Yes, joy! Expectant to enjoy the day with your children can brighten your attitude and mood for the whole day. For instance, if you're a working mom and your boss got a little over exerted in his or her approach about how you handled a situation or maybe just how a situation went about. That could and would sour anyone's mood for the day. If, you go with an expectancy of looking forward to picking up your children from school, the babysitter, or a family member, it can brighten the rest of your day and give you something to look forward to. Certainly, because our children naturally brighten our day.

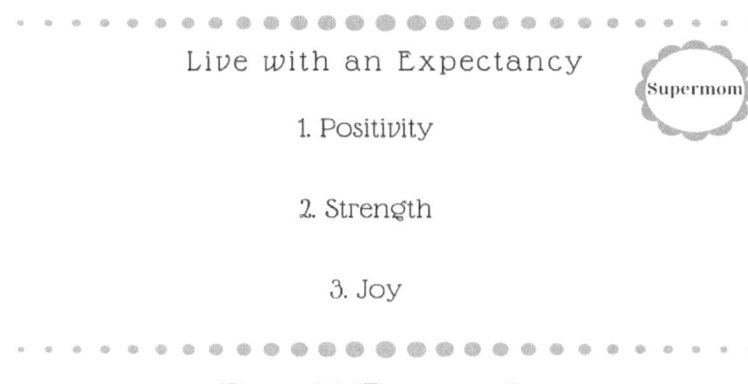

Figure 4.1 "Expectancy"

Routine for Your Loves

A routine can be vital for our infants and small children. We need to schedule routines for different reasons. For example, your young infant needs a scheduled routine so they and you can get a restful night's sleep. However, it's not as black and white as that though. All children do not run the same. Their internal clocks are all different. Keep in mind that it may be slightly harder or easier. It depends on their internal clock and the strong will of the child. Meaning, will he or she demand their way or the highway. It is easy to see the type of personality your child has within the first month.

My oldest son was very strong-willed. It took me almost three months to get him on a schedule I needed him to be on. He did not approve of the schedule. He let me know just how much he didn't want to be on it. I wanted him to be on a traditional schedule. The traditional schedule, up in the morning and sleep at night. He liked to be sleep during the day and fully awake at night. The total opposite of what I was used to.

It probably would have worked if I had a graveyard shift at work. However, it truly wouldn't have lasted long even if I did. The future of our infants' rest upon helping them establishing a routine. Going to school would be a hard adjustment time wise if they had the type of schedule my son wanted.

Once you get your child set up on a routine to your liking, it's a good idea to communicate this routine schedule to whomever may be caring for your child for any given period you are away from them. I know, some parents go overboard with the obsessing over the directions for their babysitter. Lots of parents do it. I did it. I'm sure I am not the last to do it. It should be done for the sake of the child and the mother. Why? It gives the mother peace of mind and the child a continuous routine. Don't feel bad for giving or reminding the sitter about your child's routine.

You Need a Routine

A routine is good for you. It assists you with being able to plan your family activities and work. More importantly, it gives you a set time of the day to relax. Have some quite time all to yourself. For instance, your child is on a routine for some time now and continually going down for a nap at 1pm, right after lunch.

Their belly is full, they had some time to play, and they are now resting sound to sleep for a good two hours, depending on their age. In that two hours of "mommy time" you can grab a bite to eat, if you didn't eat with your child. You have time to meal prep for dinner, wash clothes, fold clothes, clean your house, relax and watch some television, or more importantly, take a shower.

Yes, I said it, take a shower. For some reason, new moms are always worried about leaving the baby "alone" while they take a shower. Especially, when dad is up and capable of covering that twenty-minute shower. If that isn't the case, nap time for your little one should mean "Mommy Time" for you, always. Once they are safely napping in their crib, grab that baby monitor and take it with you into the bathroom so you can peak in on and keep constant eye on your little one. Remember baby monitors can go anywhere. To the kitchen perhaps or into the living room with you so you can get your soaps in while the baby is sleep.

Feeling Lost in the Routine

You are in that routine you have set forth that works for you and your baby. Are you doing things during your "mommy time" that make you as a woman happy? Are you going through life as a stalemate? Living for what must be done and not for what makes you happy as a person can be detrimental to who you are. As women, we tend to give all of ourselves to our families. You see this in moms across the board.

The "new mom," the "pro," and the "grandma." Not thinking of what will make us happy. Always putting our children and spouses first. For example, going through your daily routines like work, taking care of the kids, the husband and house chores.

Did you notice anything on this list that states doing something for yourself? It was all for others. In which, is never a bad thing to do for others. However, when you give your *all* to others it takes away from you and can cause a lot of havoc you may not realize. I noticed this happening to myself.

Losing myself in my family and work. It happens to the best of us, not realizing that its happening, especially if we are givers. As a giver or "people pleaser," we have to work hard at making sure we don't let this happen. Too many of us have gone on with a sense of unhappiness because of it. It is only the fault of us. We should learn to say no and know that it's alright to do so. At some point, we as women must find that balance.

Try thinking of a list of things that you enjoy. To help you with your list I am going to share my list with you. Here is my list: getting my nails done, going for a bike ride, shopping, writing, reading, getting a massage, and going to a movie. Let me clarify. When I say shopping, I'm speaking of "kid-free" shopping. Yes, I will say it again. Kid-free shopping! It is the very best!

Not that we don't love our children. But, when you have as many as I do, they can drive you crazy while in public a little more than usual. In public spaces kids like to turn it up a notch. Granted, not all kids kick it up a notch. But, just when you don't want them to will be the time when they will.

> *"I had children. I didn't move to Mars."*

Speaking from personal experience and other mothers that I know, we all experience this feeling at least once. Waking up thinking, "Why shouldn't I take some set time out for myself? I had children. I didn't move to Mars." You will be happier for it. When you're happy, your family is happy, in the general sense of speaking. I am not saying go throw your money and time away. I am just saying keep yourself in mind when you go through your to do list. Don't let the list be full of everyone else's needs without yours on their as well.

Chapter Summary

- Living with an expectancy of *positivity*, *strength*, and *joy* can be a great key to success.

- A routine can be vital for our small children and infants.

- Establishing a routine is also good for mom.

- Getting your *"mommy time"* is a great way to staying healthy for your kids.

- Make sure you don't lose yourself in your work and family.

- You had a child, you didn't move to Mars. You are still you!

PART TWO

Celebrating All of Who You Are

5

Owning Supermom

The idea of being a *"Supermom"* scares and even irritates most mothers. The stigma that it carries is that of having super human strength. Most mothers don't consider themselves worthy of such a title. Well I am here to tell you, you are worthy. Why should we let that word intimidate us? We do a world of things for our children, that doesn't when they are eighteen. It may die down a little as they start to get older and start supporting themselves, however, we are always there for them for emotional support.

Consider the tasks bestowed onto the women who have children.

1. The ability to *bare* children.
2. The ability to *care* for them.
3. The ability to *comfort* them.
4. The ability to *love* them.
5. The ability to *teach* them.

Now there are some moms who did not do task number one. That is perfectly fine. Why? They were given the ability to *adopt* a child that for whatever reason their biological mother couldn't continue to do for them. The circumstances for which a child cam to be do not need to affect them. The importance of the matter is the child was given the opportunity to be loved, cared for, comforted, and taught by their adoptive mother.

I truly believe those who chose to became mothers through adoption are just as super human as those who raise their children. You are super humans who sought out those opportunities. You embraced it. Not because you physically couldn't have any. Although, that may be a factor. You were given that seed inside you to be one that nurtures those children whose biological mother couldn't. God knew you both needed each other. He turned what was meant for your harm into a blessing for both of you.

Considering all the things mothers do for their children, we should celebrate being Supermom. Our children are proud of who their mothers are. They show us in the way they treat us.

Don't get me wrong. I do understand the fact that children sometimes do not show their unconditional love in a way we would want them to. For instance, the drop off at school. Your children are too cool, to give mom a kiss because you are in front of the school.

"Can I have a kiss?" — Mom

"Mom, not in front of my friends." —Child (x- the amount of kids you have)

Our children do see us as superheroes. Especially, when we are showing them the best of us. What we need to be conscious aware of is the fact that we are here to teach our children so they can learn from us. We also need to be open in learning from them.

Our children expect a few necessity things from their parents. In which, is *love, respect, fun* and *happiness*. Of course, it is not necessarily in that order. If you were to do a little experiment by asking your child what they think they should have of those from us first, fun would be their number one answer next to happiness. Why not? They are kids. Kids do not want to be serious 24/7. Adults do enough of the everyday seriousness of life.

These aspects of *love, respect, fun* and *happiness* tie in together for anyone in life. When they are properly given, these items in life are great. Life does happen and we as parents need to take it as it comes. Explaining and comforting our children when they need it.

Our Kids Needs

We were given the "super" task to give our children what they need. Yes, they need everything they expect from us and more. Our children also need things they don't like very much, boundaries and knowledge.

In raising our children, trying to instill the necessities can be a challenging task to say the least. Kids have their own mind and certainly want to do what they feel is right. With guidance and support, teaching them to respect others should be a task that we are willing to conquer.

So how do we teach our children what so many adults seem to forget? Traditionally, everything is passed down from the mother. In which, makes our job a hard one. If we stay focused on showing our children how to behave with our actions, it should not be too difficult to conquer.

We Are Supermom!!

Considering how our child learns will help you know how to take on any task at hand. The best way to add to that is by your actions. Your child see's, analyzes and commits to memory everything that you do. A thought that doesn't always stay at the front of our mind. Accompanied with what you say, you will instill everything you want them to learn.

Showing them your love will plant seeds in their heart no one can ever take. However, it will increase their heart and show them how to love others as human beings.

You may even teach them some things you may want them to forget because it was not your intention. It happens.

However, it is important when the time comes they see mom acting out of character, for you to remember you're human. Explain as best as you can and apologize. Let your child know you are not perfect and you too make mistakes. They will respect you for being honest. Especially, later in life should that thought cross their mind. Remember, you are their first teacher. All lessons start at home and continue outside of the home.

Chapter Summary

- Own who you are "Supermom" and all that you do for your family.

- Our children naturally see us as super heroes.

- Our children expect the four necessities from us from the start. *Love, Respect, Fun* and *Happiness*.

- We were given the "super" task to give our children what they need.

- Lessons start at home first.
  - **We are Supermom!**

6

Managing Motherhood

The question everyone seems to ask when they find out I have four children, is "How do you do it?" At first my answer for that question was always "I don't know. I just do." You may be asking yourself why such a vague answer? It's simple. I never knew what I was capable of until I was faced with it. As of lately, I have really been homing in on the why and how I do it. It has really depended during my spiritual journey this year. In the deepening of my spiritual journey, I now understand it to be because I was given the ability to do it, plain and simple. God doesn't give you more than you can handle. What He gives us is what we need to move forward in life to do His work and build our character. When we think, we can't handle it, it is in that moment we should be leaning on Him.

Although, I never expected I would have a huge family, I wouldn't change it for anything.

I do understand what role society tries to place on us as women and mothers when we are out and about with our children. They tend to ask mothers a series of questions trying to pry out answers for whatever they feel is justifiable to them. For instance, "How do you handle the meltdowns? How do you manage having three plus kids?" These are just a few questions I have personally have encountered. Just as if they are setting up mothers for judgement on their part. Unknowingly, so many of us mothers answer genuinely not knowing the malicious intent behind the questions.

We mothers answer the questions without thinking we are being bated by this stranger. Only to be led into a discussion you will not want to partake in. What kind of conversation am I talking about? The type of conversation that has judgement written all over it. The kind of questions the enemy wants to use to illuminate self-doubt onto an unsuspecting mother. For instance, questions that go a little like this, "Oh, you have three kids?" As the stranger looks at you with the face with their nose turned up.

"Yeeeees." —You

Why shouldn't we partake in these types of conversations? It's not so much the question that is the problem. It's the action with the question. The body language so to speak. The way the person in whom is asking the question is looking at you when they ask.

Do they have a nice disposition? Are they asking you with a lingering look of joy behind their question? Do they have a snarky reaction to your answer? Yes, people are curious. However, curiosity and being nasty are two different things.

Conversations with other people about how many kids you have can sometimes lead you to being judged by your people who have not walked in your shoes, but are willing to judge you. The best way to counteract this type of conversation is to become more aware of the discussions and where the conversation is leading. Becoming more aware will help you in the long run. Sparing any sort of resentment towards the ones who chose to be judgmental. Not allowing for people to openly judge you for being a mother and how you manage your motherhood is key.

I have had many a time where I felt like I was being judged by women who have not walked in my shoes. As soon as I got too far into a conversation I didn't realize it was going, I soon starting feeling like these random strangers were trying to judge me for the blessing God gave me in my big family. Coming from being an only child, I have always wondered what it would be like have a large family and siblings. Now, I'm able to experience it through my children. I see the closeness they share and pray daily that it will continue well into their adulthood and after I am long gone.

What I had to learn was to stop those conversations before they started. Not allowing them to step into my space and place judgement when they simply just met me. I also began taking action against those conversations and feelings. What do we do? Instead, of allowing them to step into your space with that negativity. All you need to do is hold your head high in *your* walk-through motherhood.

Being a mother is a full-time job. It doesn't matter the number of children you may have. Whether it be one child or four children. The only difference between mothers and the number of children they have is the amount of money you spend for the necessities of life will be higher for a mother of four than a mother of one. For instance, as a mother of four, having one of my children in a travel basketball league will be higher than a mother of one. It's all because of family size.

I would have to pay more money out to go travel to different locations for my whole family. In which includes my husband and the other three kids, my son that will be playing this sport and myself. A mother of one child will only have to pay for herself and her husband. The cost would be lower for the one mother. Essentially, proving that it cost more for a parent with multiple children.

Quality time spent with your children is more important. As a mother of four children myself, I had to learn to balance everything in my life. My walk-through motherhood started off a little hectic. Simply because I had three of my children throughout my college career. Shocking, yes very much so for most. There were no dorm halls for me. No overexerted party's here. My parties were all kiddie parties. I will say it was fine with me. If I were in a different head space at the time, not so much reclusive, perhaps it would have been different. I was happy with how I was and what I was doing by accomplishing my goals.

It was sheer determination to give my children and my family a better life that kept me going. I obtained an AA degree with a two and half year-old son and a baby on the way just a month after graduation. A year and a half later during the start of my last two years of college, I had my third child.

One of the proudest moment I felt was when all three of my children watched me graduate from a four-year university. My story isn't the first like this. It will not be the last you will hear of either. The determination of a mother is nothing to compare to.

As mother's we hold the keys to our families. It does not matter whether we start early or late in life. We are equipped to manage and maintain multiple tasks and duties. For example, being a full-time mom, full-time employee/entrepreneur, nurse, teacher, psychologist, the list goes on and on.

> *"The determination of a mother is nothing to compare to."*

A great deal of mothers spend their lives rushing through the day from task to task. They never have the opportunity to sit down and relax. It's easy to get trapped in by the everyday errands and chores. As these problems and tasks arise in our personal lives we need to ask ourselves a question. Why am I running myself ragged?

Running yourself ragged will not benefit you or your family in the long run. Take a moment, go over your entire schedule. See if there is a task errand you can delegate to someone else to free up some time on your watch.

Just the other day as I was going over the monthly bills with my husband he suggested we tally up our individual bills. Of course, I agreed. But, it dawned on me that when I think of "my" bills, it's not my personal bills I think of only. It is my personal bills along with the household bills. Isn't that what we do as women and mothers. We think of the whole enchilada piled on with double cheese and topped with olives and scallions.

That's where the importance for us to have our own separate enjoyment comes in. We need to learn to compartmentalize all that we do. We wear so many hats, that we need to learn how to use them wisely. In a way that will benefit us and not run us into the ground. Our job as a mom is not to meet every need our self. It is to make sure that our kids' needs are met.

If we need to call in someone in our tribe or our "sisterhood," then so be it. Have them run an errand so you can take your kids to that outing. Your kids will still be happy & you will be happy you didn't run around like a chicken with your head cut off so to speak. That is a great way to make use of the community you have built around you and your family. Also, a great way to get all that is needed to do done.

I understand the thought of letting go and letting someone help can be daunting at times. But, as I mentioned in Chapter 3, that is a great way to release some stress that will eventually harm your health if you run yourself into the ground. *Knowing is only half the battle.* Knowing that you need help or some time to yourself for a couple hours. *Doing* is the other half of the battle.

The "Bad" Days

Motherhood is not all strawberries and cream. We do have bad days. Remember, you are only human and you will have bad days. It's perfectly alright to experience those. It's how you manage to pick yourself up from that bad day that counts.

Try not to down yourself so much during your bad day or days. Yes, I said days. I seem to have more bad days around one time of the month. Every month, rather than any other time of the month. You may certainly be different. However, I have noticed the specific hormonal changes during my cycle alters my tolerance of the mundane things. For instance, being too short with your answers to a common-sense question. When we are compiled with stress and hormonal changes it is imperative to react in the best way possible. Finding ways to help alleviate your overall mood will help in how interact with not only your children, but, with those around you.

Not all women may experience it just as me. However, there is too much to say that we all don't have significant hormonal issues during that time. I have never been one to deny the truth to the "PMS" during my cycle. I am just more aware of it as I get older and my children are young.

During those short times of the month, there tends to be a *mom-kitchen* strike at least once every two months during my "bad" days. I feel that in those instances it is perfectly alright to feel the way you feel. We don't have to necessarily explain to the children what is going on. I find that it is very healthy for me to go through a good talk with my husband accompanied with an adult drink to calm the nerves. Speaking for myself. Drinking one adult drink occasionally to calm your nerves doesn't hurt.

Don't abuse it and you will be fine or simply find something that will work for you. Whether it be a cup of Camille tea or a glass of warm milk if it is what calms you.

If you don't have a husband to talk to, take a deep breath, call up one of your girlfriends and talk it out. It helps to get all the frustration our when you talk to someone under any circumstance. But remember, when they need that bending of ear be there for them as they were for you. Nothing hurts more to be in any type of relationship then one being only on the receiving side and not the giving side.

Chapter Summary

- Hold your head high in your walk-through motherhood.

- Quality time spent with your child is most important.

- "The determination of a mother is nothing to compare to."

- There will be "bad" days. What counts is how you react to them.

7

"Health includes all aspects of the word. Mind. Body. Soul." ~Shevaughn Desirée

A Woman First

There comes a point in motherhood where you realize that "hey, I was a woman before I became a mother." Usually, it happens when you feel overwhelmed by everything that comes with being a mother. The busy schedules, working at home or out in the workforce, keeping up the household chores, etc. Whether you are a *Stay at Home Mom* or a *Working Mom,* the stigma that is placed on mothers regarding going out and having a good time is one that society places on us. Being judged for how many times you go out is not the stigma we need placed on each other period. It just harms ones' psychological view of herself and how she thinks she should behave as a mother.

Granted it isn't a "free-for-all" excuse to treat our children badly or conduct ourselves in a non-respectful manner. Like my mom used to say, *"make sure your acting like a Lady."*

Treat yourself to some fun. Just make sure you're not disrespecting yourself while doing it.

In mentioned in Chapter 3, "keep yourself in mind when you are going through your to-do-list. Schedule some "girl time" with your girlfriends who also have children. Call it *Moms Night Out* or whatever you want to call it. Just remember to have a good time. Nothing is better for a nice regeneration of your spirit is some good old' time fun.

I used to have a terrible time with that thought. I was a first-time mom, that already did not have a massive social life. I never did. It wasn't something I thought I had to be, the "party girl." So, when it came time to have a baby, I didn't think I needed to focus on that area very much. However, many a time I resented not doing the adult things. It was something I had to work on. The not feeling guilty for taking my time out for myself. I still work on it.

Becoming a mom and making sure your role as a woman don't get blurred is hard work for most moms. Some moms it does not fade one bit and to those women out there like that, I always tip my hat to. Over there years it got easier for me, once I let myself lose control a bit. Yes. I said lose control. Not in the sense you may be thinking. I like to be in control of everything in my life that I possibly can have control over. Ha. That is not very realistic and over the years I have realized how much I was flawed in that area. Yes. I have since worked on it. I had to. I am a mother of four children. Can you imagine if I didn't work on it? I would be a total wreck. Stressed out, micromanaging my life without giving myself some time for me. *We are women first.*

It is important to remember that, but also to incorporate it into our daily lives. How? Doing for us just as much as we do for others is a great place to start. Start using those babysitters you have in your community, if you haven't done so already. Schedule yourself a movie date, wine tasting, shopping day. Whatever tickles your fancy. Get you girl time in. It's refreshing to hang out with the girls occasionally.

If the girls can't go when you really need you some adult time away, take you some adult time away with a special someone on a date. The whole idea is for you, mom, to break-away from the routine of raising the kids for a couple of hours. You need to regroup when you start feeling like this. *A less-stressed mom is a happier mom.*

Mental Health is Important

When I am feeling like I need some time away for a couple of hours I try to ask everyone on my list of babysitters to see who is free. I start with the people I know who are closer to me and don't have a far drive. Ranging from my mom, mother-in-law, and my sister-in-law. If my need for time alone is strong and they're unavailable, I go to the alternative babysitter I should hire. It's important to me that I take care of my health and my sanity. Heck, sometimes I even wait for the kids to go to bed and then I do a self-care regimen that doesn't require me to leave the house.

> "When mom is happy, the whole family is happy."

You may be wondering why I mentioned my sanity. Yes, my sanity is a part of my health that I need to think about. We all should. Why do I consider my sanity separately from my health? Because, I am considering my mental health when I think of my sanity. It's important to not only take care of our body, but our mental health as well. The last thing we need is to have a break down because we didn't take time out for ourselves. It can happen. Statistics show people having mental breakdowns all the time.

It is a part of who we are as women that usually doesn't come first to mind when we are single and dating or even married without children. Why? Because we usually are already taking care of our mental health without us realizing it.

I'm reminded of the times when I had only myself to think about. I took no time to think particularly about my mental health. I was happy enough to take care of what I needed. I paid my bills, I paid for my college, worked & made sure I did things I enjoyed doing. Whether it was treating myself to one of my favorite things or to some relax time by grabbing a message. As we become mothers we do the opposite. We spend time thinking of our family.

Loving Me

Loving me first is not a selfish idea. As some may think its self-fish idea for women to consider themselves first but, let me tell you it's not. *Loving ourselves is essential to us loving others.* I have always felt it's important for women to love themselves. As I think about how important it was for me to think about how I was showing myself some love. I had to think about the way I love my self, the way I am showing my daughters how to love their self and the way I show Gods love through me to others in whom may not be loving themselves.

I realized I felt like mentally I loved myself, but, I had some insecurities in how I felt others should love me, even when I became a mom.

I was a new mom, and as each new mom stage I had, I had to consider why I had these insecurities in how I loved myself. Did I truly love myself or was I just going through the motions? As I continued to listen to my inner self, I realized during my journey that I wasn't showing myself enough self-love. I started to focus more on me & my inner desire to grow in my faith and in the word of God. It was then I realized I cared too much on how others saw me &

perceived me as an individual and as a mother. I did not want that.

It was something that had festered from childhood and I had not realized that it did. It was opened to me in my daily devotionals that I needed to work on as a woman first, for me to become the woman I was made to be, for myself first then for my children. As the days went one, my self-love grew. It wasn't something I said to myself as a ritual. It wasn't something I would practice to "be." It wasn't the act of saying "I love myself," as if I was trying to convince myself of the idea. It was only the act of growth in the word of God. Simply giving more of me to Him by expanding my knowledge of Him, He gave me the love of myself in being confident in His love.

It was amazing. My self-love grew incredibly because I stopped caring about what other people thought and cared more

> *It is through Christ, that I love, for He is love.*

about what God thought about me. It turned into wanting to please Him in my actions on a daily, into showing His love to others the best way I could. It was also a great way for me to show me how to love my babies more than I could already love them, if you can imagine that. Because having children already grows an incredible love for them as soon as you see them it's an incredible feeling you never experienced.

Chapter Summary

- Taking time out for yourself is great, but remember it doesn't give you full range to do a 360 on your family & responsibilities.

- "When mom is happy, the whole family is happy."

- Health includes all aspects of the word. *Mind. Body. Soul.*

8

"A Love Unending is unparalleled."
~Shevaughn Desirée

Unending Love

Our world is compiled with different aspects *work, family, school, college, society, church, friends, community,* and so on. If you were to ask every mother how long her list was she could more than likely go on for hours. I for one have been asked that very same question by many. It is within my answering that question as I listen to myself talk, that I realize how long my list is.

In any mother, asking that same question, she can always hear herself go on with her list, that she probably never took time to see how long it is. Focusing on our long list can be daunting to say the least.

The most important item on any mothers' list would be family of course, at least we hope. We all know not everyone places that at the top, that's for a different book. Wink. Wink. The point of the matter is we all need to work and provide for our family, point blank. Whether you are self-employed or employed by someone, or a stay at home mom with husband at work. It does not make a difference. It is just how your family dynamic works.

The Stride

What keeps you moving? What's your reason for striving for your best every single day? Your reason to get up in the morning is not your occupation. It's the *love* for your children and your family. No matter the size. *It's yours.* When we have our children, it drives in us a special change. If we are fortunate to recognize this and act upon it we are off to a great start. It takes some people longer to recognize that our children are what drives us.

Our children make us want to be better people. An example of this would be having our children wanting them to see us in a good light. As a great parent. We strive daily to achieve this goal we set for ourselves. There will be ups and downs. Parenting has a learning curve. We don't start off knowing what to do or expect.

All we can do is hope our child will see the *love* behind our actions. That they will see that you are Supermom, *faults and all.* Never mind the fact that you have made mistakes. They see it and it doesn't matter. What stands alone is the love you show them.

It recalls a conversation I had with a mom to one child significantly younger than my children. She mentioned that she had some difficulty with her child and the way they were behaving. As she went on about how she felt in respects to her whole dynamic in the situation, feeling as if her child or her spouse did not understand how it hurts her when they don't notice what she does for them, how much it takes for her to do such things. She said that sometimes she cries.

I asked her did she ever express her feelings to them? She said no. Then I proceeded to ask, how will they know how you feel? She said they should just know. I shared with her how will they know if you've never expressed yourself to them. I asked her a question. Do you let them see you in that vulnerable state? She once again stated she never let them see her cry about how it hurts her. I told her if they were never to see you cry, how will they ever know you hurt too.

I shared with this mom, how this concept occurred to me once upon a time. How did I expect my children to know when I was hurting if I never let them see me hurt? No matter how big or how small the hurt is, they need to see it. You are only human. We experience more than just one emotion. Why should we not let our children experience this? It's perfectly natural to experience all emotions. That's how we were made to be.

When our children are capable of understanding that their mother truly does experience more than just one emotion, it teaches them how to respond accordingly. Bringing them up in a world such as ours today, they surely need to understand how important it is to express themselves in a controlled environment, such as your home, so when they go out into society they will understand how to express themselves properly to others.

Example. Being able to tell someone at school, when you're not around, if they are being bullied or socially ridiculed by their peers is certainly a situation you would hope your child would have learned to express their hurt appropriately so they can receive the help they need before it gets out of hand. We are our children's first teacher. But, if they were not taught at home first, how do we expect them to respond.

A Love Unconditionally

An unconditional, unending love from their mother. A love unimaginable prior to having children. You can try to imagine it. However, it never lives up to the amount of love in your heart once you see that precious baby. An unending love that seems to multiply for every child you have. Equally, I will add.

Coming from an only child family, I didn't see the love multiplied until I had my own children. My mother did show me the unending love a mother has for her child.

As personalities are different as people are different, in mother and child relationships, our bonds may also be perceived to be different. However, the underlying core in all mother and child relationships is the "Love." If you were to ask all the different personality type mothers, they will all have the same answer. They love their child/children unconditionally and unending.

> *"Love is patient, love is kind. It does not envy, it does not boast, it is not proud."*
> 1 Corinthians 13:4 NIV®

That is the pure beauty of being a parent. Not all people get to share in that special gift given to parents because they're not a parent. It is that very reason as mothers we need to take a step back to regain our focus so we can keep our eyes on our special gift and blessings.

Chapter Summary

- The most important item on a mother's list is her family.

- What keeps you motivated?

- An unconditional, unending love is unimaginable prior to having children.

PART THREE

Bridging the Gap

9

Our Views of Each Other

The way we view ourselves is important. Just as it is important on how we view other women and mothers. Our own perceived notions can cloud our minds when we haven't taken the time to get a clearer picture of what is going on. Sometimes as we look at each other, we must be sure we are not placing judgment on each other before we have all the facts. How we view other women can be passed down to the next generation through our actions seen by our children. Let me give you an example. If your view on stay-at-home moms is not in the best light you are prone to speak out loud about it. You show this by your actions towards these mothers and how you truly feel about them. In all instances of how you express your feelings about them you will be doing this in front of your children. Giving your children first hand cause to not like the children who have a stay at home mom and to not like their mom. Directly influencing your child's thoughts and feelings.

Sure, I know this may be an extreme case. Also, continuing with that example, there is also a reaction that people don't consider when they do this. Your child could also wish they had a stay-at-home mom. You may have caused an indirect result of your misjudgment causing resentment towards you being a working mom.

That's never a thought is it. If you were to have this misjudgment of women in whom you don't really know, just because you may have some slight resentment yourself.

Let me give you a real-life example. When I pregnant with my first son, I was asked by someone whom was in a better position than I was at the time was I now going to stop working and stay home with my son. At first my initial reaction was that I was insulted. How could they think I could stay home and not do anything?

Ha.

Yes, I have since grown since then and my thought process with this subject is different. I always knew there is more to just staying home. However, in my situation at that time, I was not able to be the "stay-at-home" mom and I was appalled that they would even think that I was.

I had nothing against stay-at-home moms at the time, and I certainly don't now. One of my good friends stays at home with her children and loves it. It was simply my situation and I simply couldn't afford to stay home and I was paying to put myself through college.

My situation at that time simply gave me a sour attitude in response to that question when I was asked. Plus, I felt like I would not know what to do with myself if I did. I've been programmed as most of us are, to work for someone rather than letting God lead me to where He wants me to be, whether that be going in to work for someone or staying home with my children.

It's important when we are reacting to situations or questions that we are leading the best example we can be. Or be prepared to explain your actions to the little one staring at you. Children of course learn by being *taught*. Telling them repeatedly a life lesson or any lesson in general. However, they also learn by watching and interpreting your actions. Trust this, your child is smarter than you think. Showing hatred for anything always comes across even when you're not trying to show it. *Hatred is taught.* It is not a characteristic we are born with.

We may not always remember our children are watching our every move. Our every single behavior. That is the very reason we need to be sure they see us *uplifting* other women. Other individuals in general.

No matter what the race or religion. It's alright to not like someone. If we are sure we don't like someone in response to an action of theirs, our feeling is justified. *It is not justified to not like someone or hate someone just because of their class, creed, or simply because of your ignorance to not get to know the individual.*

> *"For just as each of us has one body with many members, and these members do not all have the same function, so in Christ we, though many, form one body, and each member belongs to all the others."*
> Romans 12:4-5 NIV®

Your children will see how they should treat other women & how other women should treat them. With the upmost respect.

An example of this is when I was with some family and friends and their children. One of the children was near me and my youngest daughter. She heard my daughter answer my question with a "Yes, Mam."

All this young child could say was "Yes, mam?" As though it was a strange thing to hear my daughter or anyone say that. My response to this young child of all of eight years old was "Yes, Yes mam." I went onto say its respectful to answer that way and she should try it one day. Then I left it alone.

But, this is what I'm talking about. My children were taught to say Yes, Mam and Yes, Sir. Now they're not perfect and I'm not going to pretend they are. So, they do not say it all the time, but they say it when it counts. Why? It was taught and observed.

How was it observed? I say it. Yes, I still say "Yes, mam and yes, sir." Why? I am old school. I think its respectful. And depending on who I'm talking to I like to show my respect.

When we start placing judgements on others it's hurtful to them and it can be hurtful to your relationship.

A great way to start showing other women a little respect is to try and see what lies beneath the surface. What is really going on with them. Often, we tend to ignore the little signs that may be showing. For instance, let's say should you meet someone and that very first impression that may not have gone well. It may very well be in result of a previous mishap to your meeting.

She may be in a different state of mind. It could have affected her whole being.

> *What is lying beneath your surface?*

Things at her job may not be going well. She may have lost her job, got in an argument with her boss. All things that can alter a person's attitude and change the way their outlook is at that very moment.

I know someone who had a significant other that was going through a transition between jobs. She had some good days and expectantly some bad days.

Going from a two-income household down to a one-person income household. Those can be very hard times for a family. It eventually got better for them as he found a career that could withstand. However, during that time her attitude and judgement could have been altered by her circumstances.

I know there have been things of what may seem small to you but at a time they were not small to me.

I went to grab me some coffee before work. The barista got my coffee order wrong. As I suspected it, I tried to trust in their system. But, she gave me the wrong drink. As I look at the scenario now, it seems so small. The barista gave me a drink that contained dairy when I asked and paid for a drink that was non-dairy. A drink with soy milk. Yes, it seems like that couldn't have ended up souring my mood.

But honestly it did.

I'm lactose intolerant and I would get severely sick if I would have drunk the drink that contained milk. Getting the wrong milk didn't sour me so much because of that.

It was the fact that I was already running late for work. To top it off my kids didn't want to wake up for school that morning, and I was stuck in traffic longer than I should have been. All I wanted to do was treat myself to a nice cup of coffee and take it to work.

I was not in the right frame of mind after the morning I had. All these underlying triggers for myself and the barista I spoke of were lying beneath my surface. If I were to meet someone new, they would not have gotten the right impression I would have wanted them to. I would have been full of attitude and may have even come off as a nasty person. If I were to meet someone on a better day, they would have gotten a more put together woman.

As I was writing this I am remind of a scripture that is a wonderful way to look at this situation.

> *"Do not take revenge, my dear friends, but leave room for God's wrath, for it is written: "It is mine to avenge; I will repay," says the Lord. On the contrary: If your enemy is hungry, feed him; if he is thirsty, give him something to drink. In doing this, you will heap burning coals on his head."*
> Romans 12:19-20 NIV®

We are not called to be judging to other women or men. We don't have the right to be condemning to others. We should practice more understanding, rather than judgment. We are to be loving to others. Opened hearted to those in need. *An example of this would be lending a hand to someone who may need it and too apprehensive to ask.*

The struggles of a parent are their own. We are not supposed to "outcast" them for their struggles. Rather than doing so, we are supposed to uplift them and offer them encouragement. Therefore, giving them the strength, courage, and rejuvenation they need to carry on.

A great way to think of it is in a Christian based theology, the enemy, meaning the devil, comes at us from every angle all the time. It doesn't matter where on earth you were born or who on earth you are. It is taking you from giving birth to God's plan on your life. This is true in our fight on each other as women. Women have been falling into this trap for decades. So many women dislike each other for no apparent reason. Giving the enemy exactly what he wants, women divided. We are all victim to having him attack us. It is time we stop this cycle and stand together as one. Giving support to all mothers and those who one day may become a mother. Showing women in solidarity in a way we have never done before.

> *"When they hurled their insults at him, he did not retaliate; when he suffered he made no threats. Instead, he entrusted himself to him who judges justly."*
> 1 Peter 2:23 NIV®

How do we show solidarity? The way we do this is by growing as a person. Changing our views of each other. Changing them in such a way, that is uplifting and nonjudgmental. Putting into exercise what we wish other women would do for us.

Chapter Summary

- Children learn by watching and interpreting your actions.

- Your children see how they should treat other women by watching how you treat other women.

- What is lying deep beneath your surface?

- We are not called to be judging to other women or men. But, to be encouraging.

- Showing solidarity in such a way that we are uplifting and encouraging.

10

Embracing the Sisterhood

A sisterhood like no other. A sisterhood of motherhood. I ask you, how many mothers do you know that are not related to you? Do you consider them to be a "sister" in that right?

A sister in a community of many. There are mothers out there that need the companionship of other mothers. No judgement, open arms, and true friendship is how we should embrace our fellow sisters. Our sisterhood of motherhood is one we should not take for granted.

Let's look at this scenario. You are a stay-at-home mom that became friends with your son or daughter friend's mother you met while at a school outing. She is a working mom of three. Being that you are a stay-at-home mom, you may be more inclined to receive information from the kid's school. Maybe you live in the direct neighborhood of the school. If there were an incident down the street from the school you and the school would hear about it prior to your friend. Why? Simply by chance. You live near the area and your friend is at work.

It takes time for any school to notify a parent of such an incident. They would have to activate their call plan to inform the parents. Being that you are home, you would be in a position to notify your "sister" on how severe or not the incident is. Your notification would give her ample time to prepare herself to leave work or decide if she should wait for further information prior to leaving. On a normal day, it could take her well up to half an hour to reach her children. Given this type of incident, you could be helping a friend. Saving her from the dreaded long car ride from work to her children.

These types of friendships in our sisterhood are needed. I was luckily able to have this type of friendship with a fellow "sister." This type of event did happen to me. I of courses was the working mom.

There was a lock down at my son's school. I had no idea it was going until I was informed by a sister of motherhood. Being the working mom, she often kept me up to date with little things that were going on. That day there was some activity down the street from our kid's school. To keep all the children safe, they locked it down. Being that my friend lived near the incident she found out first hand because she was also told to stay in her home.

The school did advise all the parents of what happened via mass message. However, I heard directly first hand and I was happy to know what happened. I am in relief nothing serious happened that day. Our children were safe.

What this experience taught me was to be that type of "sister" to another mother. The bonds we create with mothers are important. I challenge you today to be that friend/sister to another mother at your child's school, at work, at church, or if you meet another mother while you're out and about.

How do you do that? How do you be that genuine kind hearted soul to another mother? Take a chance on friendship and a new sisterhood that can grow right in your own community.

Building the Bond

Here are some small steps that can lead to the beginning of a new bond between you and your fellow sister of motherhood.

1. <u>Open Up Conversation</u>

Opening up a conversation between you and another mother you have seen in passing. It can lead to a friendship you can build on.

2. <u>Look for Commonalities</u>

Common interest outside of your kids can assist you with building a tighter bond with your new sister.

3. Opposites

Be open to her if you don't necessarily have a lot in common. If you can easily get along well with each other and don't necessarily have any commonalities, you may discover you like hanging out with her anyway.

4. Have Fun!

Have fun with your new friend. Schedule some girl time away from the kids. It's good to get out of the norm meetings and hang out with your friends.

5. It Doesn't Hurt to Try

After going down this list, should you find that you still can't find where you two can be friends/besties, remember at least you tried. The idea is to be open to meeting new people, new mothers to build communities with. There are other women out there that know who you are. If they ever need a hand, you are there.

Start living a life where you view other mothers as "sorority sisters" in a club you were blessed to be in.

Random Act of Kindness

Being kind is the simplest form of a blessing we can bestow onto a sister. A sister that can come in all shapes and forms. Kindness is a wonderful fruit of the spirit that not all people choose to express on the regular. Why? There is an act some people play when we pass another person walking down the street. Granted we generally tell our children to not talk to strangers when their young. But, have we ever thought that act of protection for their safety would close them off to being genuinely kind to someone.

It seems to be in our society this generation has placed boundaries and markers up on keeping people out. Where the simple act of kindness cannot be expressed. And when it is, it is such a foreign aspect people are always shocked you were kind to them. I have always been kindhearted. But, I know I not perfect and I too have fallen victim to passing by someone and not speaking. Why? I don't know. For most of my like thus far, I have been too shy to connect with other people. There have been times where I was walking near someone and instead of saying hello I just smile.

Haven grown up in a place where there are so many people moving along with their day that passing by someone and not speaking doesn't even seem like a bad thing to do, that it fit in my once shy personality. Talking about introvert, that was a topic for me for some time. But, I will say the Lord has since taken that away from me for the most part. I haven't noticed any issue with that so until He brings it up again, I will work on other things that come to surface.

I myself love to lean on the fact that my God given personality shines bright and when I shine the light on others it just may brighten up their day. For instance, I shared some of my talents of designing some simple labels and docs for someone special, someone I like to call friend. A mom of four just like me. Made this friendship cool. It was my first ever. Yes. I said ever. Usually, I'm the only one with all the kids. Most people I've encountered had maybe one or two.

This being a new friendship that was built within the last year or so my friend continually showed me how much my light shined. How? When my friend found out I took time out of my busy schedule to think of her and make her something she was appreciative of my work and she hadn't even received it in the mail yet. But, it was something I did because I knew she wanted something like that because of a conversation we had about a similar project of mine that I did for myself.

It was her expressed gratitude of my kindness that showed me how I can express the love of God through me. Another time I expressed my love and kindness to someone who didn't expect it. Why? Only God knows why they didn't expect it. I surely don't. However, it has been something I have done for many times to those close to me. Showing them kindness because I genuinely love to do so.

As I go through the days I find myself more and more wanting to express to those who I encounter the love of God, by giving them a smile when I walk pass them. A hello ma'am or sir as they pass me walking through the grocery store. A simple and genuine act of kindness so that they may go about their day with a better vibe about themselves. Have you ever heard of yawns are contagious? I say smiles are contagious.

It's been proven. When we even lighten our facial muscles up around others by expressing a smile we don't know that may be the only one they may see that day. Not truly thinking how much a simple act of kindness we could do for someone whom may be going through something could certainly change the course of action for that day. When you smile, who knows the next step to being kind is not that far away. Show some of your random act of kindness to a fellow sister, it could pose as a first step to something great in both your lives.

Chapter Summary

- You are in a sisterhood of many.

- The bonds we create with mothers are important.

- Take a chance on a new bond of sisterhood.

- You were blessed to be in community with other women, step out and reach out.

- Random act of Kindness goes along way.

11

One Mother at a Time

Many times, when we think of people that annoy us or just get on our nerves we think of them with a sense of duty. A duty that we think is all our own. It's our duty to change them into what we think they should be. However, realistically if we tried we'd just ended up hurting each other because we would be upset they didn't want our help and they'd be upset that we didn't appreciate who they are. There is an old saying. It is said that if you want to see a change in someone, you must change yourself first. Why? You can't change someone. They should want to change themselves. The only control you have is over yourself. We can't control others' actions, nor should we want to. Just as we raise a child to do and think for themselves, we cannot force someone to do and act as we want them to. When our desire is strong to do so, we must look within our own selves and start from there.

Often enough when we really dig into ourselves we can find some things that could use some work or a change our point of view. And that is where we should start. For instance, when I was in college I was still a little negative thinking. Always taking the pessimistic approach to all things. But, the thing was I didn't realize I was being pessimistic.

I was a sociology major and had taken the approach for a criminology background of courses that accompanied the required sociology courses. Well, when I was taking a course that required me to interview some people I was really expecting a certain round of answers. Right! Of course, you would expect to have a variety of answers you imagine in your head when you think of the possibility of answers.

One of the people I chose to interview was a coworker of mine at the time that I would call friend. She said she would let me interview her. She was someone I thought was super cool, someone I'd know I would get a great set of answers from. A friend that even showed up to my wedding.

During my interview, she flew by each question I asked without any trouble. But, before we hung up, she told me she was hesitant to answer my text about doing the whole interview in the first place. I was stunned to this answer. I proceeded to ask her why? She told me because I am always negative and she was trying to not be around people who were like that. Needless to say, I was shocked! Appalled even at the thought on how could she think that about me. Really? Did she know who she was just talking to. I'm the nicest person there is.

Well, yes, I am the nice person. I am generous whenever I need to be, without thought. But, in that time of my life. I was always negative. I had many around me that had the same approach in some thought processes. Until I had this large slap in the face so to speak, I didn't realize how bad I was. I was going through life with the reality and thought process of my situation is bad and I can't do anything but complain about it and think negative about the whole world around me.

As we know, we cannot go through life thinking this way or behaving in a manner that is unbecoming of who we were meant to be. The thing we can do is start from within and work our way outward. There is an upside to remember. When you see change in yourself, little by little, they will start to see a change in you and then proceed to changing themselves to be more like you or so they say.

I would say that this works for about just over half of the population. What does this mean exactly? It means some major news here. Are you ready to hear it? *Be the change you want to see in the world.* It starts with you and who you are. If you treat other mothers like they are a part of your "sisterhood," as I mentioned in chapter 10, they will start doing the same.

Just brining up in conversations with other mothers, you will see they feel the same way. Who knows you may spark something in them

> *Be the change you want to see in the world.*

that will challenge and change their whole world for the better. They may not even have known what exactly they were looking for until that spark was lit.

In lighting ones' spark, just as a roaring fire spreads, she will be able to light a spark in someone else. Before you know it, you will have sparked a forest of women to encourage and uplift all those around them to broaden their communities/sisterhoods of strong mothers and strong women.

To inspire a change in our world, we cannot stand by and wait. We must put forth a plan of action. Why? Someone may want to know where exactly they can go to meet with other mothers. Mothers just like them. Wanting to take action and build a community where all mothers stand together in prosperity.

Start a group for moms in your area. A physical group or a virtual group such as a page on a social media site that you can manage. Set rules for this page. People who join in should be respectful of the other moms in the group. Also, set rules on whatever else you'd like to. The key here is to get everyone socializing respectfully of each other's individuality.

If you are a little apprehensive about starting one. Follow me. I have a group on a social media site, The Supermom Haven. A safe place for moms to share their feelings, ask for advice, give advice to the other mothers without judgement. You can find it on Facebook. I do manage all the commentary and the people who join in. I am hands on in the things I involve myself in. I believe strongly that we as mothers set a standard for our sons and daughters. I strive every day to show them to be loving, not only to one another but to all. I will say this, so far so good. My children are doing what my husband and I are teaching them.

The Supermom Haven is in its beginning stages and has some activity. I love where I see all the mothers giving advice to someone in need. Opening the line of communication that they need at that moment. That is what it's all about. Building up each other. Assisting other women/mothers. Letting them know they are not alone in this life. It just warms the heart to see the love in the world. We need more of it.

Remember everything starts at home. We must set the tone in how our children behave. Yes, we may have our bad days, where exhaustion sets in, we don't want to even get out of bed because we are sick, but we cannot let that define us. We should celebrate all of who we are. That is the only way we will ever grow into who we were truly meant to be. Supermom! Master of all. Child of the most high. Wife. Mother.

Daughter. Sister. Friend. Chef. Housekeeper. Nurse. Chauffeur. Taxi Driver. Personal Shopper. The list goes on and on as we surely know. With all the many different hats we wear, we cannot let that detour us from our path and purpose.

Chapter Summary

- Be the change you want to see in the world.

- Build a local community of mothers who are looking for the same thing.

- Remember everything starts at home with you.

- Looking for ideas? Join my Facebook group, The Supermom Haven.

- Don't let an off day detour you from your path and purpose.

PART FOUR

Mom to Supermom

How to start dreaming & living to move you forward into a life you want outside of your roll as MOM.

12

"All you need is a Dream in your heart to take you where you want to go." ~Shevaughn Desirée

Dream

Defining true happiness and being happy with who you are is a major milestone. It doesn't matter if you are 21+ or younger, the question always comes to us when we notice we are seeking more *from* ourselves or *for* ourselves. As a mother, it may also come to us as we wonder what life course our children will pursue. Either way, if you are thinking of a dream you may have in your heart, or perhaps you just have a curiosity about what your life's purpose may be, it takes some effort to figuring it out. If you were someone in whom you thought possessed special gifts such as Albert Einstein or Pablo Picasso, finding your purpose as a woman other than being labeled as "just a mother" would not be very hard.

Studies show that finding your life's purpose can be more satisfying and motivating than just any old job or pay increase. I too have had those thoughts as a woman and mother. Am I doing what I love? Am I fulfilling my life's purpose? I start going down my mental checklist so to speak. I am happy when I think about God giving me the ability to love and to be free through Jesus Christ. I am also happy that the Lord has blessed me with my family and health and waking up daily growing in his word makes me happy. But, sometimes I can't help but to think when I am alone in my thoughts am I truly happy?

Yes, as I said before, I often thought about this topic. Why? I had a deep feeling I still had more to grow & a purpose greater than what I was already doing. What I realized is I'm not truly happy. Not because I'm not blessed because I am. But, because I'm not doing what God put me on this earth to do.

He gives us so many dreams and aspirations. But, when we let those fall by the wayside that really has something to do with how we feel inside even in our soul we're not happy. Maybe with the friends that we have or the lifestyle that we have or think we should have. It really has only to do with us and our obedience to God.

I have been writing this book for about two and half years. Technically, not the complete two and half years because of "writers block" and the not wanting to do it because I didn't believe in myself. For a long time, I did not believe that God could put this in me. The wanting to be a writer. The craving deep inside to write, share my experiences, and help others through my writing. Why? Because I didn't go to school for writing so how could I do it. On the contrary, I can do all things through Christ and so can you! He would not have put this dream in me to see me fail. I am the only one who can make myself fail. But, when we allow doubt to creep in, those are the thoughts that try to overwhelm our minds and hearts. It wasn't until I found the strength in Christ to surpass those feelings. *If it's not for you, the door to that opportunity won't open.*

It is through Christ that I have found my courage to be *brave* and to brave society in writing my book. To be content that I have had this desire placed in my heart ever since I was a little girl. A desire to write that has broaden over the years. To be brave that I have something to say and that there is someone out there that needs to hear it. In having the desire to change the world one mom at a time is what I am after. To inspire those to provide a service to others so they may help others broaden their horizons. To help build the movement of strong women and strong mothers in their communities.

Change Is Good

It all started with a dream that was placed in my heart to help women not feel like I have felt. All the snickers from women, the "lookie loos" from women placing judgements on me when they have not walked in my shoes. Granted there are things that other women do that I will never understand and vice versa. But, it's not my job to understand why life experiences make us go through different

> *"Behind every man is a strong woman waiting to break out, so let her."*

things. If we have the desire to change, it doesn't matter how we start or how we used to be. All that matters is that we're growing and that we want to make a difference in the world and we want to change as an individual.

It is said that in order to change another individual you must change yourself first. It is a saying that is very common. The other individual will adjust themselves to compete or keep up with you. To feel they still have a commonality with you.

Have you ever felt that way? Wanting to change another individual without looking within first. We've all been in that same predicament of wanting to change a partner or someone we know. I too have thought that same thing.

When is "Sally" going to change? Granted I don't know a Sally, but, you get the idea. I have look for people to change many a time. But, the result is always the same, they don't and they never will unless it is something they want to happen.

What do you in that situation? Nothing.

You can't change someone else. You only have control over your immediate actions and behaviors. I can tell you this, it is beneficial to look within to find out if there is something you want to change about yourself.

I will also tell you right now when we are looking for change it's normal for us as human beings that we would be looking outward first. It is the very first thing we think that needs changing.

Steps We Take

Have you ever considered taking a yoga class or going back to school for that degree that you didn't finish? Thoughts and ideas normally come in a time of our life when we are looking for more. Looking for personal growth. Growth is always a good thing.

Like any other person out there, I looked at myself and said there has got to be something I can do for me. I do a lot for other reasons. For instance, I'm a mom. My kids love to have a social life. I take them places, I run the necessary errands. I take my kids to most of all the party invites they receive. You get the picture. But, I asked myself, what is it that I really want to do? What can I do to benefit me? I started to really dig deep into my inner self. Going through my dreams and aspirations to live a better life. Now I am not saying my life isn't great having a job and being a wife and mother, but, it can always be better. You can always be better. *A better version of yourself.* Isn't that what we all want to be, a better version of ourselves?

What that means for you may be different from what that means for your neighbor, coworker, friend, or family member. Although, we may have some commonalities with the people in our circles it doesn't necessarily mean we are the same. Each one of us mothers has super unique gifts within the multi-layers of placing others ahead of our own self. We just need to tap into them if we haven't done so already.

Is there a dream that you have been putting on the back burner? Or maybe a dream that you try so hard to come to fruition and it just didn't work out. Maybe it wasn't supposed to work out, it could have been the journey of trying that was the purpose. Everything happens for a reason. Whether it's to help you learn something, for you to teach someone else or it may have not been the right time for you to fulfill that dream. It may have just been for you to learn a skill that you need to use for a higher purpose.

As I speak these words through this text, in being completely transparent, it took some life lessons for myself to learn before I could understand this idea completely. It was as if I was learning another language. I had to go through the steps of the lesson to get to the answer. As in a traditional class in any school setting, the teacher gives a lesson and the student must practice in doing homework and study prior to being tested on the material either that same week or the next week.

With life, it works the same way. You are given times to practice, times to study and times to take that test. And some lessons you may not get the first time around. I know I had to take some test more than once and I'm alright with that now. As I went through them though let me tell you it was a hard lesson as I have a hard head and may have not understood what was going on at the time. I now understand that it was the journey that accompanied the lesson I needed to learn. With life lessons, sometimes they can make us stray from our purpose in life if we are not learning from them, we are repeating them. They can even do damage to our self-beliefs. Making you think you don't have all the tools within you to achieve such goals and desires in your heart. I am here to tell you that you have what it takes, it just may take you through something rather than to something at first. To make it to those dreams and desires you need to know yourself and dig in to your soul to see what part of the journey they are a part of.

Recognizing the Dream

Recognizing our dream can take but a few steps. For example, the following list can be taken into consideration when we go down our list of recognitions.

1. What am I good at?
2. My Intuition
3. Have I tried this before?
4. Is this worth my time & effort?
5. Am I letting myself control my destiny?
6. Am I going after this for just money purposes?
7. Is there a time limit I'm giving myself to see if this works?

Now let's get a closer look in to these seven questions we can have to figuring out our dream and how we can recognize where it stems from.

1. What am I good at?

Looking in to your skills is a great step to take in recognizing your dream. I always like to look at my skills as I write them down as sort of a starting point to see what I know. Then I like to make a list of what I've been thinking of that has me in this market of consideration of what my dreams are.

Many of us have a lot of skills that we build up over the years because either we have learned them through the jobs we have had or by taking courses to learn something new. Heck, some of these skills may have been built in our high school years. For example, I have known how to type since my tenth-grade year in high school. Yes, way back when they use to offer typing classes as an elective for people whom where a business major. It's a skill I built up for many years.

I have also built up skills in the food industry because of the jobs I've had for many years. Skills I love and come in handy when I need to plan a birthday party for my kids. Why? Because I can whip up some party trays with no effort at all.

Once my compiled list is complete with all the skills I know how to do, I like to sit and use this time to decide if I am searching for a job, a career, or simply some time to myself where I may need a new hobby to pick up.

2. My Intuition

I like to use my intuition in making my decisions. Sure, using the usually list making, logical thinking way is great sometimes. However, some people use it and still fill like they haven't a clue to what is truly bothering them. I myself have felt that. It's a natural thing to do.

I usually feel this way during a transition period of my life. As soon as I have compiled my list together of what it is I'm skilled at. I usually like to sit and marinate on the idea of transitioning to another career. Because let's face it, that is usually what is bothering us. A completely and totally common aspect. However, there are those times where we may be feeling like is it my job or career that is bothering me. Or is it the fact that I may be lacking something in the other areas of my life.

That is why it's important to use our intuition and tap into it. Some people may have a feeling they get when something that is near that gives them what they would call a bad vibe. For example, I always get this feeling deep down in my gut when something isn't right. You may be different in how you receive your intuition. But, no matter how you receive it, the best way to develop it is to keep in tuned to it and it will grow stronger. A great thing to remember is your intuition was placed inside you to keep you from danger or to follow a certain path you should be on.

3. Have I tried this before?

Many may consider doing some things in life because it seems familiar. Familiarity can be a *dream crusher* and a *life stealer*. Why so harsh? Let's look at this example. When we stick to what seems familiar we are less likely to try anything else. Sometimes those things that are unfamiliar and uncomfortable are better for us. For example, my family and I recently moved to Texas. A state we have visited before and I love when I visit. However, I have never lived there before. I was a born and raised California girl.

With life, sometimes things just aren't great for you. It all came down to struggling to raise a large family in a big city with layoffs and no jobs to keep us a two-income family. It was tough to say the least. However, with constant prayer we kept feeling like we wanted to move to Texas. There were more promises that we could see that could happen for us but it was unfamiliar for me and my children. For a few years of trying, it just didn't seem to work out.

I heard the Lord speak to my heart and tell me to lay roots down at a church I was currently attending. Well, like all people who think they know better than Christ, I questioned Him. I kept asking Him why? Why do I do this if I want to move and feel like you are telling me to move. Then I heard Him speak to me again, which was great because I know He doesn't always speak to you after you question Him. He told me again to lay down roots they're at my church The Church On The Way in Van Nuys, and so I did. I laid down roots at the church. Trying to step out of my comfort zone again He spoke to me and said to plug myself in and be open.

If you ever knew me, that in itself was hard. I did just that out of obedience and felt like He would not steer me wrong. I was right. After a few years at the church my husband and I finally felt like we couldn't take much more of the high price of living in the big city. So, we prayed and prayed and prayed. God answered us and my husband went out first, landed a great job immediately and I followed with the kids. Our eyes were opened to the promises He told us would happen if we finally trusted Him and stepped out on *faith*.

I did something I had never done before. I went into the unfamiliar and left. I left everything, my job that I had for years, my vehicle, my family and friends. I followed Christ to where He wanted me to be. Unconventionally, at that. I am such a planner if anything ever stepped out of my plans/box, I would freak. Christ brought me to a whole *new level of me*. He answered my dreams because I trusted what He placed in me to do.

> *"If you are willing and obedient, you will eat the good things of the land."*
>
> Isaiah 1:19 NIV®

4. Is this worth my time & effort?

Making sure something is worth your time and effort can be a real-life saver. There is nothing worse than wasting time and effort on tasks and things that don't do anything to make your life better. Like does that argument over who's the best employee really get you anywhere. No, it doesn't. But, there are other ways to fight back in that arena and others. Take the old saying, kill them with kindness. Kindness is in short supply these days, why not spread more around.

Are you in a place where your time and effort are appreciated? Are you feeling like you, mom is being appreciated? Sometimes we feel that way. It starts to show in how we feel and how we feel we should spend our time. Are we spreading our time and effort on everyone but us? Those are timeless questions from women and mothers. Make sure you take those into account when you are going through that list.

5. Am I letting myself control my destiny?

Control is a very strong word to me. It seems like daily someone is trying to control something. That's why it's good to ask yourself am I letting myself control my destiny and my life? As moms, we can let other things take control of every aspect of ourselves because we take on too much and don't delegate when we need to. It can become overwhelming and controlling of our lives.

Another aspect can be when we as women and individuals let other people's suggestions override our better judgment. For example, if you are questioning whether you should go forward with a project and you ask someone for their opinion. If their opinion is strong enough it can cause you to second guess yourself and leave you questioning more than you were in the beginning or it could persuade you to go the route they picked instead of you taking control and deciding for yourself. Now don't get me wrong, I'm not saying don't ever ask for an opinion. But, when it concerns your future, its better left off as you are making the decisions for yourself than someone imposing their ideology on you.

That's why I love helping my clients. In our coaching sessions, my clients are completely responsible for making their own decisions. I just provide them with the ear, the safe place to speak, and the ability for me to help them clarify what they want to be asking thought provoking questions.

6. Am I going after this for just money purposes?

A timeless question when it comes to finding our dream and purpose. Are we going after a career or job for just what we think the money can do for us? Rather than being content in what we want to do whether or not the pay is going to make us rich. I know there are those of you reading this thinking how can she say that. I love making a great living. That's awesome!! I am not questioning what you do for a living. I am merely saying that when we find ourselves consumed in what a job can do for us because of the money aspect we often find ourselves unhappy and resentful because we followed the wrong pursuit.

When we follow the pursuit that is going to make us happy regardless of the pay we are better off. Sure, we need to make a substantial amount as parents to be able to provide for our families. In my own experience, I know I rely on the Christ to be my provider. Also, I rely on my efforts to meet Him half way. Faith without action is not good. You must show how much you want something out of life.

> *"So you see, faith by itself isn't enough. Unless it produces good deeds, it is dead and useless."*
> James 2:17 NIV®

7. Is there a time limit I'm giving myself to see if this works?

The age old saying, timing is everything is true. I like to say all in Gods time. But, when we are trying a new career, a new hobby, any kind of new transition, we can give ourselves a time limit right? I believe time limits are a good thing. They prevent you from wasting time on something you may have decided is no longer worth the time and effort you are giving it. In considering setting time limits on anything, be sure they are comfortable to you without going overboard by procrastination. Depending on the task, a usual good time limit is a week for small tasks and it goes up from there for larger tasks. Setting a healthy time limit on tasks is a great way to keep you moving toward your goals and dream. Procrastinating the outcome can leave you feeling afraid of whatever your outcome may be and prolong you from moving forward in life.

Chapter Summary

- If it's not for you, the door to that opportunity won't open.

- Change is a good thing

- Familiarity can be a dream crusher and life stealer.

- Don't be afraid to become a new level of you.

- Kindness is in short supply, why not spread some around.

- Setting a healthy limit on tasks is a great way to keep you moving toward your goals and dream.

13

"Believe in your ability to have the life you really want."
~Shevaughn Desiree

Believe

Believing in a life we want can be a daunting task for some of us women. Adding the factor in when we are mothers is another area we want to feel fulfilled to how we think things should be. When we are searching for our dreams and desires, knowing them is not all we need to do to make sure they come to pass. *We need to believe in our own ability to make them happen.* It is not enough that we want to these dreams to happen. Believing in them is only half the battle. The other half the battle is that we need to put it into action. For example, in my circumstances let's take in to account that I love the fact of moving to a new city to own a home with a lot of land, a large home, and a price that does not blow my mind.

I physically and mentally know that if I want this, I must believe that God will get me there. However, I must also put my words into action. I should also prepare to make my dreams come true. For example, I must pursue a career in that state if I can't transfer from my current job. I must look in to the housing market in that state and take the necessary steps into purchasing a house. Those are the actions steps that go along with my need to pursue a different lifestyle and produce a lifestyle change for myself and my family for the better.

Why is that? Like I mentioned in chapter 12, *faith without action is useless.* I need to put my words into action. I can't just believe it will happen, I must take what is called *S.M.A.R.T Goals* towards what I want. What are S.M.A.R.T. Goals? S.M.A.R.T. goals are *specific, measurable, attainable, realistic, and time bound* goals to keep me moving forward in life and not stuck in a rut so to speak. Setting smart goals help to hold myself accountable. It does help when we can have an accountability partner like a coach to help us get to those goals we want to achieve. What does a coach do? They help pull out what is already inside of you. An important task they have. Helping you realize you already have what it takes to get to where you want to be.

What if you're lacking in the confidence? What if you are unsure of the steps to take when you are just figuring out you let yourself be consumed with your family and not giving yourself what you want? What then? Continue to believe in your ability to make a change in your life and the lives of others. You are the one in whom can make it happen. Know that I believe in you!!

What Is Worthiness and How Does It Affect Me?

The definition of worthiness is having worth or value. Worthiness is a key ingredient to our belief system. When we are feeling unworthy it can be hard to believe we can accomplish a goal no matter how big or small the goal may be. There are several categories as to what we tell ourselves as to why we aren't worthy of an opportunity. For instance, here is a self-doubtful saying I hear all the time. "I haven't gotten any skills in that arena, what makes me think I can just up and pursue a job let alone a career anyway." Well, that may very well be a fact. You may not have any skills in that arena you are thinking of pursuing. However, it doesn't mean you are not worthy of it. It doesn't mean you aren't worthy of trying. Like I tell my kids all the time, just because you've never tried something doesn't mean you can't do it. It for dang sure doesn't mean you are not worthy of receiving your heart's desire.

There are a few reasons I'd like to point out as to reasons people say to themselves that they are not worthy of going after their dreams and desires.

*Reasons <u>We Say</u> We're **NOT** Worthy:*
- We were told for most of our lives that we can't do it.
- We don't have the necessary skill set to get the job done.
- We have low self-esteem.
- We get complacent in our current situations that we give up on a dream we think will take more effort than we are willing to put in.
- We say we don't have the financial resources to pursue a new endeavor.

When we are told for most of our lives that "you can't do that" or "you don't have what it takes." It can really attack your mind, soul, and your body. Why? We start believing the lies that other people are telling us about what we can and cannot do. It becomes the soul and dream crusher on our lives that leads to low self-esteem and becoming complacent in our situations. I try to teach my kids all the time how to talk and communicate with each other in a manner that is uplifting to each other. I tell them it's hard enough to battle what is going on outside of our home, that our home cannot emulate what is going on outside. To remove the "you can't do that" from their vocabulary and replace it with a phrase suiting to the situation. For instance, when my youngest son and my oldest daughter get into a disagreement. Being the big brother that is literally 15 months older, he likes to use the "you can't" phrase a lot when he feels she's not doing something he deems to be correct. So instead of using that I taught him to use a phrase that is like "do you want me to show you how to do it so you know next time you can do it yourself."

Now that phrase doesn't always work of course. Like I said its depends on the situation. But, I told him by rephrasing it, it doesn't tell her she can't do it. It's showing her that he is there for her when she needs him. It also shows her that if she's not sure how to accomplish something instead of feeling bad about it, just ask for assistance so she can learn and try again later on her own.

He understands how when we as people speak those types of words to others that it's hurtful and debilitating to their growth. I taught him and my other kids that those two little words can send our lives on a course we don't need to be on. But, by using encouraging words and phrases we can set up others for a lifetime of inner strength that they can continue to build on.

Reasons <u>We</u> ARE Worthy:

- We are the children of the most high God and He has given us a purpose and talent to fulfill.
- We are *strong* women and have a duty to our young *successors*.

- We have *love* for *ourselves*.
- You are worth more than gold.
- Our dream is *bigger* than our doubt.

It is our God given right to pursue the dreams He has placed on our hearts for His glory. Not all dreams are to come to pass. We know this. Some are placed inside us to take us through the journey to gain the lesson to take on with us through life. But, if we let those feelings of doubt sink in we will never know what is supposed to work and what is just for the journey lesson all because we didn't believe in our ability to change the world.

Not all women go through life thinking of our young predecessors. We may only consider this when we have children. However, what if you had only boys? Aren't there any young women or young lady's in your lives? Young lady's that are family members, or young lady's you are connected to through work, friends? Don't we owe it to the next generation to lead by example and show them how to proceed or not proceed in life? We do. You are worth more than gold itself, believe that.

We are constantly being watch by our young ladies. How we talk about and attack our dreams, goals and desires are being watched considerably on a daily basis. Those young ladies can learn from us and see the strong women in whom we are, whether we think so or not. Our love for ourselves can be just the very start in leading other women to their destinies and we don't even know it.

The Value of You

Just as we can consider the ideas and knowledge of what worthiness is, we must understand our self-worth and how society defines self-worth. Self-worth is self-esteem and how we feel about ourselves and whether or not we have a value. Society defines self-worth by what is in the mainstream media. Which is not always a good thing. Our self-worth must be on our terms. How strong and proud we are of ourselves and not letting what someone else's thinks of us.

Look at the movements that have been taking on in society recently. Standing for equality and respect for us a person and not for what people think we should be. Defining our own terms and not letting someone or something define our future and success. For many years women have let men and job success stem from what they think we should be by such terms as letting them call us out of our names. Now I know not all people have let this happen, including myself. But, it doesn't mean that it didn't ever occur. I was reminded of a song I grew up listening to in the 90's that was so empowering for young women such as myself that demanded the respect from men and other women as to not let them treat you any other way then with respect.

It's uplifting to young women and women in general. Giving you a subliminal message as to assist you when those instances occur. You have a place to draw from and empower you without even noticing. For instance, I was working with someone new in my department. I was a mom, a wife, a woman of age, and this young guy came into this place of employment and thought he was hip and cool and decided to call me a B***h. Yes, I said it. Right. I told him kindly not to address me in that manner, I am not that kind of girl that thinks its ok to address me as such, never have and never will. He tried it again and that's when I had to lay it in with a stronger voice and with an attitude that if he didn't stop he would not like the outcome of calling me out of my name. It was then that he stopped.

Just think though. If I was not secure in who I am. If I did not realize my value as a woman, I would have let him do things that were unacceptable in my book to treat me the way he was trying to treat me.

It's a time and age as to have seemed to be taken on a whole other light today. Where did it go wrong? Was it by those of whom what have allowed others to devalue who we are and what we can bring to the table because they were afraid of being the one to stand up for what they believe to not be acceptable in their eyes? Or is it because they did not believe their value to life and society was bigger than what they could see? There are small steps that can be taken and they have already begun. The movements that have swept the nation as to not allowing people to continually devalue your humanity. It's an important step to believing in yourself and your capabilities to contribute to a better you and a better society.

Mindset is Everything

I love it when I am having a great day. When my hair is on point, my skin is looking amazingly clear, my makeup looks great, and I feel absolutely sexy!! My confidence is on a natural high. Isn't that just it though. When we are experiencing these great days of feeling and loving our *self-worth*, it's easy to have a great mindset. What about the days when we aren't feeling that great. How do we keep believing in our ability to move forward with our goals?

I like to try some steps just as simple as to listening to a song that may help me get pumped up for whatever I'm about to do. A song that brings great feelings to mind and happiness to help change my mood around in which turns my mindset around.

Haven't you ever listened to a song that may come on the radio and you think to yourself of a time that may not have been a great reminder of what you used to be. A time that you thank God for having to go through to get to the place you are today? I love those times. Why? Because they remind me of my continual growth and how far God has brought me. But, let me say this. I would not have grown as a person if I wasn't open to all of what God had for me. The steps of changing my mindset was one of them. I know in my own heart if I wasn't open to changing my mindset, I would not have come as far as I've come.

Change Your Mindset to Lead You Forward

- Decide that you need to make a change.
- List what you want as a result. *A Permanent Result or Temporary Change.*
- Research groups that are of value for the mindset changes you want to make. *This will allow for you to have some support & they may even provide Mantras to assist you in the mindset change.*
- Do things as to fake your brain into thinking you already have the life you want. *For instance, a vision board, to help assist you in already seeing the outcome you want before it happens.*

These are just a few ways to assist you on a path of a mindset change for your life. That will lead you in believing in the person you are and the dreams yet to be discovered. In fact, I also have compiled some very realistic and mom worthy, business woman mantras of my own available for anyone with the desire to taking the next step in mindset change.

Chapter Summary

- S.M.A.R.T. Goals keep you moving forward in your destiny.

- Complacency can keep us from saying we are worthy of more.

- You are worth more than gold.

- Your value is far greater than what another person says it is.

- Mindset is Everything!

14

"Go out & Live the life you have always wanted."
~Shevaughn Desiree

Live

Life takes us through things we weren't expecting at times. What matters deep down is how we bounce back from those unexpected situations. Completely understanding how we react to those unexpected situations in our lives is essential. No one person has it all figured out. Sometimes it takes us more than one occasion or situation to teach us what we need to know. However, once we do, how do we go out and start counteracting those unexpected situations? How do we start living the way have sought inside our inner selves once we understand what we truly want? We start with the list we came up with in our steps to becoming all of who we want to be. I have found that in truly living our dream in excelling in the area we want it requires action on our part.

In those actions, I have gone over my desires and believes and then I must place them all on a list. Whether it's a paper list or digital list, in compiling yours, it's up to you. Whatever is easier for you. I on the other hand, prefer to compile any type of list, ideas, down on paper. I'm a little on the old-school side even with today's technology. Once we've come up with our list, our idea dream of what we want to do and we have the courage to go after it, it's time to put those ideas into action. It's time to start living those dreams and desires.

Focus

In focusing on your new perspective towards the future and your goals, you need to remember to take it day by day. In any area in life whether we recognize the patterns, it is beneficial to move in a day by day manner. Taking time to enjoy the life we were blessed to be given. I know it can be a hard task for some, including myself at times, but if we are honest with ourselves, it is easier to move in to acceptance.

I like to remind myself of a small but mighty perspective. Every day I encounter people in my daily walk, how I represent myself will outshine all in any given moment. So, I remind myself that *"I am the Light & the Life."* It doesn't matter what everyone else thinks of me. If I am focused on how I am representing the Lord, all else will follow through. I will be the *Woman and Mom God made me to be.*

Living Life

I have now dreamt big! I now have the mindset that will take me into new heights. All that is left is for me to start living it out. Putting into action the goals that you have set forth for me is that place to start. But, how do you do it? "There has to be an all in all, tell me exactly what to do and I will do it exactly in that way." Well, let me tell you everyone has that thought every now and again. I know in my mind that I need to dream, believe and live a life I love. I know to do so, I must set goals to get me there. But, as human as we are, we get nervous. If the nerves get a chance to gain life, like anything else they will fester and grow bigger than they need to.

Let me give you a great example of nerves gone haywire. I used to be a dog owner. After they pass and gone, I tried to own another dog, shoot I even did. His name was Kobe. Yes, he was named after a celebrity. I was unable to keep him any longer in the small place my mother and I lived at. The next best thing was to find him a great home and we did. Well, after years of not having a dog, literally almost twenty years, I found myself a mother to four and somewhat freaked out near dogs. German Shepherds to be exact. A little background on why I was freaked out near German Shepherds. At the age of seven I was on my way to the park with my aunt and I was attacked by a German Shepherd. I had to be placed in a cast for one month. I broke my right collarbone and couldn't move my right arm and had to sleep on the floor because of the cast.

I eventually healed and later had trouble carrying the massive books in my backpack when I got older because my collarbone area hurt on the same side of the one I broke. Years went by and I had not realized how freaked I still was about those types of dogs until the day I had to walk and pick up my kids from school. As I walked to pick up my kids, I saw a stray dog. A dog non-other than a German Shepherd. I got extremely nervous. I didn't see the owners nearby. I hadn't even seen a collar on the dog. The dog looked well-groomed though. I tried to wait near by a postal carrier I saw near his truck. Thankfully, he was grateful I told him about the dog because he hadn't seen him. He alerted me to wait awhile, try and give some distance between me and this dog.

As I felt that maybe the cost was clear. I saw another pedestrian. I went on with trying to do my duty as a mom. I ended up seeing the pedestrian go another route and saw a gentleman nearby outside his home. What did I see? The man also looking at the stray dog roam about the neighborhood. I happened to mention why I stopped in front of his house. I was so nervous, I called a family member that lived a couple blocks away. I could not let the chance of that dog getting near me and sensing the nerves and fear that had seemed to fester inside of me all in about a ten-minute time frame.

I know by me exposing my most vulnerable and crazy nerves gone haywire I am leaving myself open. I don't care one bit. I know that if I can help one person, I'm good with that. In fact, it's therapeutic for me to be writing this. I had not known that I am still extremely nerves when it comes to those types of dogs. I had no clue that would ever happen. I thought I was fine. One instance as a child had lied dormant for so long, how would I have ever known. By me telling you this, it is a perfect example of how if given a chance to gain life, like anything else, nerves will grow bigger than they need to.

Having nerves never hurt anyone if they don't gain life like I've just mentioned. In fact, being nervous about doing something new can be a sign of a step in the right direction. It means you are off to a great start. You are stepping out of your comfort zone and expanding your horizons. That is always a good thing.

A great example of healthy nerves is, for instance, taking on a new job or career you have prepared for and have been wanting for a long time. You will experience a little bit of nerves on the first day of the start to something different. As moms, we also know that our children also get a little nervous on the first day at a new school. It is perfectly normal to experience those types of nervous.

Stepping out on faith takes some embracing the nerves and stepping into the life that was meant for us. So, how do we approach this living the dream, taking on the new and exacting things we want to try? Whether they are career change or simply an empowering stage of our life we must focus on the goals we set.

Here's how we do that by setting goals and trying our best to stick to them.

S.M.A.R.T. Goals

Specific goals are used and needed to lay our ground work for our ideas and whether it is beneficial to what we need to be doing.

Measurable. How do we know if the goals we set are measurable? We measure our goals by understanding what we want. We need to find out how they pertain to our overall plan we have decided upon. We need to think about if we can narrow down the goal in to smaller steps.

Attainable. Are the goals I set for myself attainable?

Realistic. Are my goals realistic to what I am capable and willing of doing?

Time Bound. These goals I have set for myself can be measured by time.

Completing smart goals can be challenging for some people and other's not so much. What I would recommend to anyone who were to ask me how do you do it? As I've mentioned in the previous chapter, chapter 13, it is best to have an *accountability partner* to assist you and hold you accountable for the goals you have set for yourself. Having an accountability partner will only help you in moving forward. When you are looking for someone to be that partner, it is best you find a nonpartisan partner. Someone who has no gain in anyway but to see you do better and achieving your goals.

Now there are coaches for just about every type of goal you have. I recommend if you are looking for that person to help push you and hold you accountable, do your research. Don't be afraid to ask some questions you may have if you are not clear by checking out their website. Take advantage of the coaches that offer a free/complementary coaching call session. This will give you and the coach time to feel each other out and make sure you are a great fit. If in the chance that they are not, don't be afraid to ask if they can refer you to anyone who may be a better fit. Lastly but not least, remember, *you are Supermom!* You don't have to be rich, in the best type of car, or in name brand items to be a good mom/parent. All you need to do is be yourself, love your children and be the best person you can for them. That doesn't necessarily mean it's by living the "status quo."

Chapter Summary

- Take a step day-by-day.

- Nerves are good as long as they aren't out of control.

- Taking Action is necessary to move us forward.

- You need an accountability partner that has no stake in gaining anything but seeing you do well.

- You are Supermom!!

Quotes to Remember

Chapter 1

"When you do grown up things, grown up things happen."
"There is no such thing as The Perfect Mother."
"Good parenting has nothing to do with DNA."

Chapter 2

"95% of parenting is leading by example. The other 5% is life experiences."
"It is our perseverance and faith that gets us through the difficulties."

Chapter 3

"We were created to be social human beings."

Chapter 4

"I had children. I didn't move to Mars."

Chapter 5

"Lessons start at Home first."

Chapter 6

"The determination of a mother is nothing to compare to."
"There will be bad days. What counts is how you react to them."

Chapter 7

"When mom is happy, the whole family is happy."

"Loving ourselves is essential to us loving others."

Chapter 8

"Parenting has a learning curve. We don't start off knowing what to do."

Chapter 9

"Hatred is taught. It is not a characteristic we were born with."

Chapter 10

"Being kind is the simplest form of a blessing we can bestow onto a sister."

Chapter 11

"Be the change you want to see in the world."

Chapter 12

"Behind every man is a strong woman waiting to break out, so let her."

"In order to change another individual, you must change yourself first."

"You can always be a better version of yourself."

Chapter 13

"Believe in your ability to have the life you really want."
"Just because you haven't tried something, doesn't mean you can't do it."

Chapter 14

"Nerves are good as long as they don't gain life and go haywire."

Afterword

"As for you, be fruitful and increase in number, multiply on the earth and increase upon it."   Genesis 9:7 NIV®

    The idea for the book came from trying to figure out what I wanted to write about. I had so much inside me I felt I needed to get out. It was something I pondered for a while. I questioned myself on what is it that I feel I could contribute to the world. Then it dawned on me. I wanted to do something to inspire and empower women to be their best self as mothers & women. For one, people were always calling me Supermom. I just didn't believe myself to be. I was always down playing what I do as a mother and my abilities.

    I do a lot for my family and I'm not the only mother that does this. But, then I thought about all the times I felt like I was being judged by other people both men and women for being a working mother of four children. I am not the first and I am not the last woman to have a huge family, "why am I being judge for doing something God gave me the blessing to do?"

      Then it came to me. Why not be the one to start a movement of women changing the way we interact with each other? Showing our children, we can lead a movement to span the world. A movement of empowerment. A movement of kindness. A movement of no judgement.

I had to write it. There was an excitement in me that needed to proceed. The Lord gave me the idea to blossom and move forth with. I was happy and scared at the same time. Starting something new is always a little scary. I mean I am just a girl from California wanting to change the world. How is this going to happen? Are people going to receive it the way I want them to?

All questions of doubt that of course would stop anyone. But, when God gives it to you, you must proceed no matter how long it takes. I have been working on this book for well over a couple of years. Stopping and starting of course many times. Looking for ways to keep me on my toes. I am blessed to be able to express myself and what was placed in me to do. I can only hope that all of you will feel the same as I do. Wanting to be women that change the world one mother at a time. I am Supermom & you are too!!

Let me take this time to extend a special offer to you for grabbing my book. If you are serious about taking yourself in to another dimension of you, I offer you *a 30-minute complementary coaching call.* Please visit my site to schedule it today to see if I can be of any assistance to you.

Bible Verses

"I took you from the ends of the earth, from its farthest corners I called you I said, 'You are my servant'; I have chosen you and have not rejected you. So do not fear, for I am with you; do not be dismayed, for I am your God. I will strengthen you and help you; I will uphold you with my righteous right hand."
Isaiah 41:9-10 NIV® ~ **Chapter 3**

"Love is patient, love is kind. It does not envy, it does not boast, it is not proud."
1 Corinthians 13:4 NIV® ~ **Chapter 8**

"For just as each of us has one body with many members, and these members do not all have the same function, so in Christ we, though many, form one body, and each member belongs to all the others."
Romans 12:4-5 NIV® ~ **Chapter 9**

"Do not take revenge, my dear friends, but leave room for God's wrath, for it is written: "It is mine to avenge; I will repay," says the Lord. On the contrary: If your enemy is hungry, feed him; if he is thirsty, give him something to drink. In doing this, you will heap burning coals on his head."
Romans 12:19-20 NIV® ~ Chapter 9

"When they hurled their insults at him, he did not retaliate; when he suffered he made no threats. Instead, he entrusted himself to him who judges justly."
1 Peter 2:23 NIV® ~ Chapter 9

"If you are willing and obedient, you will eat the good things of the land."
Isaiah 1: 19 NIV® ~ Chapter 12

"So you see, faith by itself isn't enough. Unless it produces good deeds, it is dead and useless."
James 2:17 NIV® ~ Chapter 12

"As for you, be fruitful and increase in number, multiply on the earth and increase upon it."
Genesis 9:7 NIV® ~ Afterword

Notes

Chapter 1: The Transition

    Facts obtained from the US National Library of Medicine.

Acknowledgements

I want to take the time out right now to thank a few moms that have shown me along the way everything I need to know. Let's start off with the ultimate Supermom that was in my life, *Dolores Reyes*, my grandmother. A single mother to six children in a time women were looked down upon for not being married, separated, and raising children on her own. She was a strong Latino woman with conviction. I am blessed to be her granddaughter. May her soul continue to *Rest in Peace*.

My mother, *Margarita Taylor*, with a heart of courage to break from the norm and raise me as a divorced, single mother, with love and all that was in her to do. I will never know the complete struggle she had in providing for me. However, I understand her right to keep that close to her. I also understand that she did the best she could with what she had. I Love you! Thank you for being the "Lita" you are.

To my mother-in-law, *Marie Brinagh*. A Supermom in her own right. She has embraced me with love since our first encounter as I was dating her only living son. Thank you for being you!

To my sister-in-law, *Chantel Steinreich*. Thank you for showing me alternative ways to parenting, parenting through Jesus Christ. Although, Jesus Christ was always a part of me, I didn't realize how to include Him in my parenting. Alternative ideas I took from you and many others, helped build me into the mother I am today.

Although, this person is not a mom he is my one true love. To my husband *Ronnie*, thank you for being my rock. I love you very much. You are always by my side and you have encouraged all my endeavors. I appreciate you more than you will ever know.

To my four children, *Omari, Matthew, Jasmine and Zoey*, I am grateful for you every day. Although you push mommy's limits, I am proud to say I am your mom. You are the best part of me. I will love you to the end of days. As my kids loves to say, *"I love you to the moon & back."*

To the women of the small group at church; *Chatel S., Mercy I., Cecilia G., Richelle K., and Kristi K.*, you all have encouraged me, prayed with me, and given me great pleaser to be a part of your walks with your children & life. I truly love the friendships that are being built. Thank you for welcoming me and my family with open arms when I was brand new to the small group experience. You all made it very easy.

To the women, I have grown to know and love through the meetings from our children at school, women of all different ages and backgrounds, *Kanah, Heather, Martha, and Miriam,* I love our talks, experiences and all around company. You are all great women in your own right. You help me stay on my toes with keeping true to what I am doing in life, bridging the gap between all moms from all walks of life. Although, we all met through our children, we are the reason for keeping it going. Love hanging out with all of you!!

Finally, to *Heike B*, thank you for helping me when I needed it. Noticing through our conversation that I had "Baby Blues" and I needed to do something about it. I don't think I ever truly expressed how much I needed that talk with you that day. As a new mom, you gave me great advise & showed me I was not just a coworker, *but a friend*. Love you!

About the Author

Shevaughn D Henderson is a Certified Women's Empowerment Coach and Author. A native to California she obtained her Bachelor of Arts in Sociology from California State University, Dominguez Hills where she concentrated her studies on urban issues.

Shevaughn is *The Supermom Coach*. Empowering mothers to dream, believe, and live a life they love. By embracing who they are and going after their every ambition. Doing it all through her 1-on-1 coaching, group coaching and private Facebook group.

She is a child of the King of all kings, Jesus Christ. Wife to her wonderful husband Ronnie. A mother to four beautiful children Omari, Matthew, Jasmine and Zoey. Her four beautiful children keep her on her toes constantly. She wouldn't have it any other way.

She loves the closeness of her family. Shevaughn also enjoys the quietness she receives when the kids are sleep or at a sleepover. Whether she spends that quite time alone or with her husband, she is completely content with her many blessings she has received.

---

sd-henderson.com
Facebook & Instagram: @iamshevaughndesiree

Twitter: @iamshevaughndes

More from the Author

Shevaughn D Henderson is set to bring her first children's book coming out late 2019. For more information on book title release information, please visit her website sd-henderson.com.

www.ingramcontent.com/pod-product-compliance
Lightning Source LLC
Chambersburg PA
CBHW021408290426
44108CB00010B/437